A WARTIME MEMOIR

HUNGARY 1944–1945

ALAINE POLCZ

A WARTIME MEMOIR

HUNGARY 1944–1945

Translation, Introduction & Notes,
by Albert Tezla

CORVINA

Published in Hungary by Corvina Books Ltd. 1998
1051 Budapest, Vörösmarty tér 1

Originally published under the title
Asszony a fronton, Szépirodalmi Kiadó, Budapest, 1991

Corvina Books Ltd, acknowledges the financial assistance of the
Hungarian Nemzeti Kulturális Alap.

On the cover: Alaine Polcz, 1944

ISBN 963 13 4556 4

CONTENTS

War is not easy. Neither is marriage.
Still, I will try to tell you how things were,
because I must tell you some time.

INTRODUCTION

"I always walk on the shadowy side of life"
– the author.

Before the publication of *Asszony a fronton* (A Wartime Memoir. Hungary 1944–1945) in 1991, Alaine Polcz was widely recognized as a psychologist ministering to the needs of disturbed and incurably ill children and their families, as the author of numerous articles and several books on thanatology, and as the founder of the hospice movement in Hungary. To those who knew her through these dedicated engagements with death and the dying, the account of her experiences in the closing months of the Second World War was a revelation of past horrors in Hungary which, until then, had lingered on in the farthest reaches of the national memory as rumor and suspicion about the violent acts committed against women during a time of chaos, havoc, and savagery. In her review of the work, Anna Földes, a respected critic and literary historian who had previously interviewed Polcz in relation to her publications on death and dying, originally thought that Polcz was led to the care of dying children by experiences not uncommon to many members of the war generation: the uprooting from her home and becoming a refugee in Hungary, the terrors of the war itself, the years of delay in beginning a professional career, the decades-long excoriation of the writings of her second husband, Miklós Mészöly, the distinguished modernist in Hungary's prose fiction, by critics and literary historians serving the interests of the government, and, possibly, illnesses she had suffered in her youth. Now that Polcz has broken out of "the tower of silence" with the account of what she endured when she was only nineteen-twenty, Földes comprehends what Polcz meant when, during that interview, she expressed her gratitude "for the trials of existence," for, as she states in her review, she now learns for the first time that the author herself had completed the "school of death, the university of trials" and passed the examination in the "relieving discipline of enduring the unen-

9

durable, of the human bond that shines forth even in hell." Földes now concludes that, because she was denied the happiness of motherhood for which she had so fervently longed, Polcz eventually chose to become "the rational guardian angel of children."

But even Polcz's very close friends were entirely unaware of the story of her first marriage and her war experiences which she so honestly and frankly discloses in this book. In his review, Ottó Orbán, the noted poet and personal friend of Polcz and her husband Miklós, observes that all that had been generally known about her was that she was for a long time a psychologist at a children's clinic dealing with their difficulties in entering the world and then devoted herself to the departure of human beings from life in as humane a way as possible. In a narrower intellectual circle, she was also known to be Mészöly's wife. As someone closer to the two of them, Orbán had, of course, heard something about all kinds of horrors Alaine had experienced during the war and also about a serious illness she had suffered; but "with the dull-witted arrogance of those who had lived through the siege of Budapest," he somehow supposed that the bombing had simply been "a bit more violent" in the area where the war had caught up with her. As for her having been sick, "Who hadn't been? I was, too. Big deal!" Orbán had appreciated the fact that she wrote her studies in "respectable Hungarian, and not in the gobbledygook of the international psychological dialect" so prevalent in that body of literature, but he found in them no evidence of an author-in-progress. There is no question that, like Orbán, even her closest associates and friends were unprepared for the revelations of the confessional and its literary quality. Even her husband, to whom she readily turned for help with her professional writings, did not see this "chapter" from her life during its long genesis until it was published. Describing his response to his wife's literary activity in a interview published on January 3, 1998, Mészöly explains: "It was always obvious to me that an interest to do such writing existed in her. She had planned for a long time to write her life's story, an account of her experiences during the war. Earlier I myself had a part in her working on her professional writings; I served like a midwife at the birth of the texts. Now, however, when Alaine embarked on the writing of *A Wartime Memoir*, I sensed she had to be left entirely on her own, that I should not participate. So, although I knew she was working on it, I did not read it until it was finished." Asked whether he was able to resist looking at the manuscript, he replied: "Yes. And I am extremely glad it happened that way, for, to my very great surprise, she created a magnificent confessional volume, in an entirely new style." The literary world quickly recognized its merits: It was awarded the prestigious Déry Prize, named Book of the Year in Hungary, and highly praised by Hungarian reviewers, and has already been translated into French, Rumanian, Slovenian, and Serbian.

Information about her life remains scarce, but fortunately, Polcz has provided some essential details about other "chapters" of her life in a radio interview on a program called "Calling Card," which was also published in *168 Óra* [168 Hours], March 30, 1993, and in "My Autobiography," a six-page account, which appeared in *Mérleg* [Scale], 1995. These articles, supplemented by her answers to questions submitted by the translator, shed some light on her life with her family in Kolozsvár (Cluj), Transylvania and her lasting, deep devotion to the place of her birth as a rightful part of historic Hungary, both of which nurtured her sense of values and shaped her view of life. She limns a picture of family poverty and economic struggle in post-Trianon Transylvania during her early years. She wore hand-me-downs and shoes with holes in their soles, and the family of seven lived in a room and a kitchen, without lavatory and bathroom. Relatives who lived in two- or three-room places with doorbells seemed foreign to her. Her reaction to hardship and her parents' efforts to make ends meet may be an early indication of the tremendous inner strength she manifests toward the trials of marriage and war that she recounts in the memoir when she says that "poverty has many jewels and joys... not known to the rich," and that human beings, while they are children, consider everything they experience to be "normal, natural" if they are, as she was, "enveloped by the atmosphere of love and joy." She delighted in summers spent in a village with relatives and friends, close to animals and nature. Attending

11

high school presented a real challenge to her: she had to maintain an excellent level of scholarship to remain eligible for a tuition exemption and, at the same time, tutored students privately for income, and helped at home because her mother, from whom she received her love of work, perseverance and sense of feminine modesty, was employed outside the home to help make the family more comfortable.

Polcz expresses indebtedness to her early years in Kolozsvár for her deep belief in religious freedom and tolerance for minorities. In the family home, in the small room and kitchen, "we were Unitarians, Roman Catholics, Greek Catholics, and Protestants. The transformations and developments of our faith – school and marriages often exerted decisive influence – we changed from one belief to another." Her father frequently remarked, laughing: "Do bring home a Jewish daughter-in-law, the family is incomplete without one." When that event occurred happily years later, and the new daughter-in-law, Ici, was serving her first dinner to the family, Polcz's younger sister, Kata, whispered to her: "How happy she is. She thinks it is something for her to wind up in a purely gentile family in which everyone is a doctor." Of course, there was such banter, Polcz remarks, but she came to know true religious conflict only in Budapest. In addition, in Kolozsvár it felt natural to be living among many nationalities. Rumanians, Hungarians, Germans, Ukrainians, Serbians, Jews, and Armenians lived side by side, and despite the expected slurs and racial jokes that were voiced within the ethnic groups, she has, on exposure to the world, come to realize what the basically harmonious relationship prevailing in that multi-cultural society meant to the evolution of her view of life and her own, open attitude toward human beings.

There was, however, another side to her life in Kolozsvár that affected her profoundly during the inter-bellum years. Transylvania was no longer a part of the historic Hungarian homeland which ancient Hungarian tribes had occupied along with the Carpathian Basin during the ninth century. When the first Christian king of Hungary, Stephen I (c. 970-1038), was crowned in the year 1000, Transylvania became a part of the Kingdom of Hungary until the Treaty of Trianon, in 1920. At the time when the Turks occupied the center of Hungary from 1526 to the end of the seventeenth century, and the Habsburgs ruled the western and northern regions of Hungary, Transylvania was governed by Hungarian princes, the famed Rákóczis, and served for a time as the center of Hungarian culture and as the custodian of the highest political traditions of Hungary. In Kolozsvár, Polcz lived amid powerful echoes of this centuries-long kinship with Hungary. Matthias Corvinus, known as the Renaissance king of Hungary, was born there in 1443. During his reign from 1458 to 1490, he strove to restore the Hungarian state after many years of feudal anarchy and became, in the eyes of many modern historians, one of the most impressive figures of the period in central and eastern Europe. His court in Buda attracted many important humanists, including Callimachus Experiens, who lived at the court from 1483 to 1484, Marzio Galeotto, who resided there frequently between 1461 and 1486, and Antonio Bonfini, who, following frequent visits that began in 1486, became a permanent resident at the court from 1496 until his death in 1502. Matthias' library, the Bibliotheca Corviniana, was the first among the libraries founded at the time; it consisted of about 600 codices, and its original titles were prepared by scribes and miniaturists in Italy, mainly Florence, and later at an illuminator and book-binding shop in Buda, where he also established a printing press in 1472. The house in which he was born and his statue still stand in the center of the city.

The ties of Polcz's birthplace with Hungarian culture are numerous. It is the place where Hungary's first encyclopedia was published, in 1653; where Miklós Bethlen, the noted 17th-century Hungarian politician and political writer, carried on his work; where Miklós Tótfalusi Kis, who went to Amsterdam to master the art of printing, quickly established his European reputation, published a controversial bibliophile edition of the Bible in Hungarian, and returned to Transylvania and settled in Kolozsvár in 1690 to live out his remaining years; where Mikes Kelemen, who, accompanying ruling Prince Ferenc Rákóczi II (1676-1735) into Turkish exile as his secretary after the defeat of Hungary in the War of Independence in 1711 and writing the letters that became a significant part of Hungary's literary heritage, received his education; and where the first Hungarian theatre was founded in 1792.

The trauma of being wrenched from their ancient historical and cultural roots by the Treaty of Trianon was aggravated for the 1.6 million Hungarians in Transylvania by the Rumanian state's policies aimed at marginalizing the minorities. The policies applied to all the minority groups, but the government, viewing the Hungarians as the most threatening to the security of the fledgling state, applied restrictive measures against them more aggressively. It curbed the use of the Hungarian language, denied written legal status to Hungarian churches and violated religious freedom. Its educational policies, aimed at the assimilation of minorities and the suppression of their educational systems, eliminated more than fifty percent of all Hungarian schools and Rumanized the Hungarian university in Kolozsvár. The government closed Kolozsvár's Hungarian National Theatre, denied the freedom to organize meetings and even required authorization to celebrate engagements, weddings and Christenings; it imposed censorship on the ethnic press and inhibited individual freedom through a fifteen-year enforcement of martial law that made house searches and illegal arrests common occurrences.

The Polcz family felt the hand of oppression directly. She writes: "I was born in Transylvania after the First World War. I came into a world in tears and mourning following the shock of having my birthplace severed from my homeland. I have a black necklace whittled out of wood, called beads of mourning. Women wore them after Trianon." It is true, she says, that she was still able to attend a Hungarian school and that she grew up in a Hungarian environment, but her father was constantly being harassed and taken away, and relatives were always spending time in prison. She was forced to learn many words and names strange to her ears and soul, and she can still remember what was etched in her mind as a young student under the Rumanian monarchy: *"Maestates sa Hohenzollern Sigmaringen Carol al doilea"* – His Majesty Charles II of Hohenzollern. Even her father's failure to register the date of her birth and his choice of her name were an expression of his resistance to the Rumanian administration. When queried about the prob-

14

able inaccuracy of 1922 as the year of her birth published in a literary lexicon, given the age at which the events in the memoir took place, she stated that she was born on October 7 but did not know the year. There were five children in her family, and none of them was properly registered at the time that they were born, because her father did not want to acknowledge the Rumanian administration but hoped that the Hungarians would soon return to Transylvania. When they did come back in 1940, as a consequence of the Second Vienna Award, and reintroduced a Hungarian administration, her parents could not decide the year of her birth, but she thinks 1924 is the more likely date. As for her name, her father chose "Alaine" because it could not be translated into Rumanian. Only in 1940 did she learn that "Alaine" was her first name. Until then she was called "Ibolya" [Violet] within the family and at school. Perhaps her father was, she notes, not knowledgeable enough in French to realize it was a name for a male, and she may, she thinks, be the only woman in the world with the name of "Alaine." She found, as she had with poverty, a valuable benefit in experiencing political oppression: being a member of the opposition, she says, gave her enormous inner strength.

Then, historical events again altered her life radically, this time for the better. The Second Vienna Award reattached Northern Transylvania to Hungary, and everything in Kolozsvár changed overnight: "Hungarian police and soldiers, Hungarian placards and newspapers, Hungarian films, Hungarian currency, Hungarian books. Hungarian is spoken in official agencies. Hungarians become the ruling class." Her family's economic situation improved vastly. Her father, an ordinary lawyer who did not speak Rumanian, became county attorney general. They moved into a four-room apartment in a villa and had a female servant, of whom she speaks fondly in her memoir.

But their elation at the change did not last long. Three months to the date of the Second Vienna Award, on November 30, 1940, Hungary joined the Tripartite Pact and entered the war. On that very night, the air-raid blackout went into effect in Kolozsvár. "We nailed carpets on the windows, and because we were young, we danced – to a gramophone wound

15

up with a crank. Tangos, Vienna waltzes, English waltzes. My mother wept in an adjoining room. Two days later, the young men were transported to the front." In a passage in "My Autobiography" that could serve as a postscript to the memoir, she observes: "One who has lived through a war views life differently. War cuts you to the quick, it strips you naked. That is, if you are caught up by its current. There are provincial towns and villages where the war quietly flows over you; you manage to swim through it, knowing starvation, experiencing anxiety, and acknowledging others' losses. I got into its very middle... I never knew anything about what was happening to me, about what it meant. I simply met my fate. Angels were holding me in their hands, but I foolishly thought I was suffering."

Polcz is responding to the horrible experiences she narrates in the memoir. At Csákvár, she, her husband, and her mother-in-law were swept into fierce battles between German and Hungarian forces and the Red Army that had broken through the Carpathian passes with the support of the Rumanian army that had defected to the Soviets on August 23, 1944, to occupy Western Hungary and join the siege of Budapest. Evacuated by German troops to Mindszentpuszta in the Vértes mountain range before the advancing Red Army, Polcz, her husband, and her mother-in-law were forced by Soviet forces to march back to Csákvár after Christmas, where the bitterest fighting was taking place between Bicske and Lovasberény, southwest of Budapest. Villages changed hands frequently, often daily; the front billowed back and forth. Trapped in that vortex of violence, Polcz suffered the horrors of war as only a woman can know them: physical and emotional humiliation, bestial violations of her very being – events which she kept entirely to herself, as she did her stressful life with a controlling husband, until the memoir was published forty-six years later.

In 1945, after the war ended, Polcz went back to Kolozsvár. She started to work as a journalist at a paper called *Népiesség* [Patriotism] while she was studying psychology at Bólyai University. In 1946, she had to leave Transylvania because of her Hungarian citizenship and fled across the border with her husband to Hungary and settled in Budapest. She continued her studies in psychology and pedagogy at Péter

Pázmány University (later Loránd Eötvös University). She had to support herself entirely while she was a student, working as a clerk at the National Széchenyi Library and later at the Children's Psychological Institute. She barely managed to obtain her degree because the communist government, declaring psychology a bourgeois subject, closed the department. She received her doctorate in the restored Department of Psychology, Lorand Eötvös University, in 1959. Radical political changes continued to plague her life. The multi-party democratic system which emerged from the physical and human ruins of the war and held so much promise for the future of Hungary could not withstand the power of the communists, backed by the presence of large Soviet forces; it was gradually subverted until the Communist Party, headed by Mátyás Rákosi, an exile just returned from Moscow, seized power in 1949 by using what came to be known as "salami" tactics. Seven years later, in October 1956, the Revolution erupted, only to be quickly and bloodily put down by the Red Army, and János Kádár was put into power as head of the Socialist Workers' Party. Polcz summarizes what she experienced in Hungary up to the present day: "... first came fascism, liberation after nazism – for that is what it was for a while – then followed communism, the Revolution, vengeance, a soft dictatorship, then the struggle for democracy within a democracy." She adds: "And two marriages, both a great and serious education." The recurrence of her illness for three years took her to death's door, from which, she says, Miklós, whom she met in 1947 and married in 1948, pulled her back. And yet, as with earlier adversities, she viewed that ordeal in a positive light; it made "life, the world open before me: the university, travels, intellectual and physical pathways. And unceasing transformation and development." In her mind, she had to develop the ability to write, to have something to say, so that she could write her books and be able to work with the dying. She had to acquire knowledge and experience, she states, elements she also needed for her work in psychology. She writes: "When I am in a bad mood, I say to myself: I always walk on the shadowy side of life. That's the way it is. During the Revolution, a tank projectile struck right below the window we were looking through – a passing episode, for the Revolution was beautiful too;

17

but during the detentions and executions my temples turned gray in two weeks. Well, this is needed for psychological experience, too. All this together is the School of Adversity. I do not recommend it to anyone, only if someone has something to do in life. But I did not want any of this, either – instead, it was given to me. I was also given things to be done."

She began her professional career by working with adult mental patients in the psychiatric ward of the National Neurolgical and Mental Hospital, using play, art, and writing as therapy, which was quite uncommon in Hungary fifty years ago. Then she treated disturbed children at the Central Child Welfare Institute, introducing play diagnostics and play therapy into its program. Next she served as a psychologist in the Children's clinic tending to dying children. After her official retirement, she undertook medical psychology and the care of dying children in the oncology section in a children's clinic of the Central Council of Hungarian Trade Unions. Then, when she was seventy, she turned to the care of dying adults and the assistance of mourners, and launched the hospice movement in Hungary in 1991. Since its founding fourteen hospice departments have been created and 1,400 persons trained to conduct its work, and the Hungarian Hospice Foundation was established, which she serves as president and which publishes a periodical. She has contributed extensively to the literature in her field. A selection of her titles indicates the subjects of her professional interests: *The Lion Cub Play as a Diagnostic and Therapeutic Tool*, 1962; *Puppetry and Psychology*, 1966; *The Use of Puppet Plays in Psychodiagnosis and Psychology*, 1966; *Effective Play Diagnostics and Psychotherapy*, 1976; *Medical Psychology in Practice*, 1987; *Our Attitude toward the Dying and the Body of the Deceased*, 1987; *Order and Disorder in Human Behavior*, 1987; *The School of Death*, 1989; and *Will I Die Too? Death and the Child*, 1993, the last two being works she considers of special value to the general reader. From such labors, she "joyfully retreated to the kitchen. I even wrote a little cookbook: *Let's Cook Easily, Quickly, from Nothing.*" She has also published *Macskaregény* [A Cat Story], an autobiographical book on cats, and *Olvasólámpa* [Reading Lamp], a book of essays, and is writing a book on cookery, all the while continuing her work as a psychologist and a housewife.

Polcz addresses directly the content of *A Wartime Memoir* and her attitude toward the war on the back cover of the third edition, published in 1995:

Every war has a thousand faces. This is mine, as I survived it. How a young woman, I myself, as a wife of a couple of months, and age 19 to 20 landed at the Esterházy manor house in Csákvár from the ranks of a Transylvanian minority, from a Transylvania just reunited with the motherland.

A woman's life at the front. Hunger, lice, digging trenches, peeling potatoes, cold, filth. This life was not only mine. My husband's whitehaired mother was dragged away and raped as pubescent girls were. Russian soldiers attacked me, beat me, protected me, stepped on my hand with a boot, fed me.

What were they like? What were we like? Why did they rape women knowing they possibly would pay for it with their lives?

Not only bombs and projectiles annihilated, not only Hungarians and Germans were killed. Why did they make war? And why did we?

Her narrative unfolds from March 1944 to fall 1945. Two strands progress together: her unhappy marriage and her war experiences, particularly during the three-month period of sexual violence she endured and its impact on her physical and emotional being. Hungarians had long been aware of the atrocities and reprisals civilians suffered at the hands of Russian soldiers, and they had heard rumors about how women disguised themselves to be spared sexual attack, and whisperings about friends whom Russian soldiers had raped. But, as Péter Balassa, a reviewer, points out, no one knew from a victim's point of view how brutally and, at the same time, how naturally the rapes occurred, in one way or another, as a commonplace of everyday life. Political considerations and official censorship kept them from being reported and out of the historical record for more than forty years. Another reviewer, Sándor Radnóti, looks beyond such censorship for an explanation of the long period of silence to a cause which, he suspects, dwells more deeply in society: "The degradation itself induces suppression. The act of rape tarnishes, the loathing falls upon the victim, too. Vulgar public opinion holds her under the unseemly suspicion that she cannot be blameless if *that* happened to her." In her review, Földes maintains that if historical circumstances after 1945 had permitted "the wounds of rape and forced sex to be brought to light frankly and objectively, and society had taken into account the not incomprehensible fury of the instincts of starved soldiers on the loose for hours, sometimes for days, the ulcer would not have turned so gangrenous." But, she adds, if times had been different, "even the objectivity of history could not have prepared or compelled anyone to crack the hard seed formed from the silence for which Alaine Polcz had need for decades."

Polcz decided to crack that seed about thirty years ago in order to console a close woman friend, now deceased, who was going through a marriage crisis, promising never to disclose her name. As the motto of the book indicates, she wanted to say that it was possible to overcome everything, even the worst situation, that one can survive a bad marriage just as she had her own and the war, "how, after many horrors, a human being can recover and find happiness in a good marriage." As best as she can recall, she wrote the account between 1975 and 1980, and let it lie fallow for some ten years. Then in 1989 she read an essay by János Rózsás in *Újhold* [New Moon], a yearbook, and, provoked by the negative image of the Russian troops it conveyed, she took up her old manuscript again, because she wanted to say that there were many kinds of Russians. Pressed for time by the demands of her profession, she had constantly struggled with the writing of her specialized books, but this one "I spoke into a tape recorder, this one sort of slipped out." She dictated in this manner in the early hours before she left for work, and the tapes were typed out by a friend, Márta Bernáth, who suggested minor stylistic changes. The result is testimony to her natural powers of narration. The memoir is written in a clear, simple, direct style. There is no embellishment of her situation, no meandering, no sense of a work actually being composed. She does not analyze or explain, and despite her profession, she does not "psychologize" her experiences. As one of the reviewers, Csaba Károlyi, opines: "Instead, she stays with an apparent naive delineation. She does not stylize or conventionalize the material, she does not lyricize, she does not turn artful. She simply enumerates the facts one after the other; she allows those facts to throw light upon her and the situation in which she found herself." In addition to the artlessness of her style, he considers a very distinguishing feature of her mode of writing to be her capacity to "relate the extraordinary occurrences that befell her without placing her own person in the foreground in an offensive way, even accidentally. And precisely because of this, her wisely remembering individuality is recognizable in her mode of turning toward matters through the discipline of her style." Balassa finds that "the novelty and greatness of the book lies in the fact that a professional writer would not permit himself, or very seldom permit himself, to enumerate only facts and events from beginning to end in a book. The unstylized fact becomes confessional, the almost fictitious narration of the facts. This is a monumental epical story that today only the literature of fact is capable of presenting." Földes maintains that Polcz's credibility derives from the objectivity of her narrative style: the objective presentation of the facts of her story "curbs her most personal confessions. This enables us (along with the author) to make moral distinctions between human beings – murderers and victims, accomplices and witnesses."

The work is, indeed, the depiction of Polcz's journey through the various levels of hell. In the span of a year, she is subjected to a succession of events appallingly brutal, forcing her to know every physical pain and mental agony, every affliction and humiliation a woman can possibly experience. Földes finds fear in its various forms to be the focal point of Polcz's narrative: "In the age of innocence one still does not know that one has reason to fear. Then one learns to be anxious, to be terrified, to tremble, and, whimpering, to leap out of a window into a shower of bullets. At first, to fear only isolation, then the rattle of weapons, mysterious noises and soldiers breaking in, starvation, the savage embraces inflicting physical pain, the undesired male strength. Fear silences not only laughter but weeping as well." For Orbán, to a woman there can be "no greater trial of spiritual strength, a more difficult test of good taste, than the delineation of her own rape."

The ultimate triumph of the work lies in Polcz's ability to feel neither hatred nor desire for revenge, even though the bestiality of her violators still haunts her dreams, and the grave illness that resulted from the bestiality deprived her of the ability to bear children. With every reason to call to account those who had victimized her, she does not pass judgment on them. She speaks of every human being in her story, including herself, as Orbán puts it, "with sorrowful understanding, refraining from the opiates of vengeance and self-deception." She is able, according to Károlyi, "to rise above her own sufferings, not through some sort of exuberant charity but through her recognition of the interdependence not only between those with whom she suffers but also between violence and victim." According to Balassa, Polcz "holds a mirror before us; meanwhile, she lives with the prerogative and superiority of the truly despoiled. She does not pass judgment." He finds her attitude a very great matter in Central Europe, that "her disclosures are not combined with a thirst for revenge and hatred." Her "monumental epic of terror points back in time" – just as the last contingents of the Soviet army are leaving Hungary – "without vengeance, and this act serves as a worthy example from which all of us can learn. Ultimate defenselessness does not necessarily or automatically lead to the destruction of love."

This capacity of Polcz's occasioned speculation about the source of her ability to rise above her experiences in such a moral act. Understandably, several reviewers attributed it to woman's temperament, to woman's outlook on life. No doubt the powerful impact of the work stems from the fact that a woman is speaking of her world here, not a man, a rarity in European as in other literatures of the world. Judit Barabás, in her review, sees as a substratum of the work "the outlook that is distinctly woman's very own, justifiable psychologically: the capacity to perceive, solve and acknowledge the concrete, the momentary occurrence and situation – the latter is frequently the only possibility for survival," and she identifies as a female attribute "the capacity to survive, the ability to remain alive," a trait which "almost automatically makes one act in situations at the brink." Balassa maintains that "the female temperament, the woman's lot is always closer to the fundamentals of nature, history, and existence. The constant, instinctive, and seemingly animal connection with ultimate issues, which springs from physical defenselessness, sexual and social defenselessness, appears here as incomplete profundity, powerfulness, and somber splendor... Present here are the recreative and cast-in-life belief and the restorative, elemental power of the female temperament, precisely because the courses of male passion, confessions, and messages are not knowledgeable in the same manner."

Ottó Orbán, who considers the memoir one of the most shocking and uplifting books of recent years, recalls an episode in his Budapest apartment in which Polcz tried to calm his rambunctious three-and-a-half year old daughter with the velvety voice he identifies with the manner of those who work with children. Stealing a look at Polcz, he mumbled to himself: "That won't work. It's one thing to be involved with children professionally, quite another to have your own child." To this day his face reddens with acute shame at the stupidity of that statement. "I did not know that a dead person was also sitting on the edge of our bed. The young woman that Alaine once was, who, like normal women generally, wanted to bear children but within whom, instead of the joyfully bursting ovum, the war rotted for long years, in the strictest sense of the word, like a living contagion." Concluding his review, he observes that, as Polcz was writing, the words of the Hungarian language "seemed to give way under her hand, and from that inexperienced hand flowed a novel that smites the chest.... I have been a professional writer for thirty years, and now its material laughs in my face," asking me: "Do you want to really know me, chum?"

THE HONEYMOON

János and I were married on March 27, 1944, the fourth year of the war, in the church on Farkas Street. Do you know the five-hundred-year-old massive Gothic church with the austere Protestant interior? I attended the Calvinist High School for Girls next door; I was confirmed and gave recitations there on major holidays. The bishop officiated. János Székely, my religion teacher, also in a robe, and my godfather, Ferenc Deák, a Calvinist minister at Hidelve, participated. My classmates in their uniforms formed a line, and my teachers were also present.

Before the wedding they teased me about how I would have to speak my vows in Latin, and Erzsike Kovács, my Latin teacher, would be there. She was, and when she offered her congratulations and embraced me, she whispered into my ear, "You may now call me by my first name."

These are my happy recollections of the wedding. But all those people. And how can I hold the train, the veil, the bouquet, and my bridegroom's arm all at the same time? I won't be able to take a step if I don't hold up my dress and veil, because they will stick to the coconut matting and pull me back. On the way to the church in the car, the best man, whom János chose, flirts with me outrageously; I do not quite understand him, and he gives me this piece of advice, "You must not do anything the first night, you will be *so* worn out; don't spoil it."

The bishop goes on unmercifully long, I am unable to follow him, it is tiring to stand. Magnesium bulbs are continuously flashing (pictures are being taken), I can't refrain from wincing.

János, utterly bored, stretches his leg (the bishop notices, I am very embarrassed). It is over. I wait for him to speak or gesture to me, but no, he looks elsewhere. At this, I somehow go limp inside. I do not remember whether we spoke to each other at all on the way home, but, in fact, we were numb; we had been so swamped by people we could barely fight our way to the car.

Then the wedding feast. Bride and groom at the head table.

When the others eat from china, silver is set before us. When they eat from silver, gold is set before us. Every dish is brought to me first; I put some on my "lord and master's" plate, then on mine. (Next they serve the bishop, then my mother.) Erzsi, our Transylvanian servant (we became engaged at the same time and waited for letters from the front together; her fiancé was killed in action), whispered to me, blushing, "Please take less." Then more insistently, "Madam says you should not eat so much." Only near the end of the dinner did I come to understand that it was not proper for me to eat so much. How unfortunate that I never asked them why.

At the sidetable, my sister and my brothers, their cronies, and my girlfriends were having a jolly time. At the head table, a dreadful boredom reigned, but my mother would not allow me join them; I think the others at our table shared my suffering.

Or were they feeling fine? I haven't the faintest idea!

Telegrams, flowers, and gifts had been inundating our home since morning. Father was the chief county attorney at the time, and it seemed as if he was going to become Lord Lieutenant; so, as was the custom in such circumstances, everyone was trying to gain his attention.

I hate sitting at the table when my stomach is full. Finally we got up, after what seemed like an endless period of time. I fortified myself with black coffee, and I was allowed to join the young people; I found my cat, which I truly regretted leaving behind, but János did not let me take it to my new home. I would have liked to register at the university very much; I wanted to become a physician, but he would not let me do that either. I acquiesced, for I loved János deeply. I met him when I was fourteen years old; he was my first love, and the first to kiss me. He asked me to learn to type, so I could transcribe his manuscripts. (He took his degree in economics; he wanted to become a writer. Four years of service at the front followed; meanwhile, I finished high school and graduated.) I studied typing, but I really hated it; an oppressive anxiety descended upon me; in the meantime, I practiced the scales with ten fingers, touch-typing.

I had just begun to feel better when they accompanied me into my old bedroom. János removed my veil and wreath, handed them to my mother, and expressed his thanks to her for me, or for the dinner, or for the whole wedding. My mother handed me over to him and asked him to take good care of me. With that, we left. Only years later did I find out that my mother started to cry, could not stop, became ill, and did not rejoin the guests.

Our new apartment, on the mezzanine of a villa, faced my parents' one-family dwelling and garden. We simply walked across the narrow, cobblestone street that ran into the hills. Maybe I would have liked him to carry me over in his arms. Or did he, only I no longer remember? How did we enter? What did he say? Did he undress me or did I undress myself? I can't conjure up anything. I simply don't have any recollection of that first night. (If Freud was right, I had reason to forget it.) A single trifle remained. During the night or at dawn, as he lay beside me, he put his leg, bent at the knee, across me, and that felt very pleasant. Everyone recognizes this movement; children are wont to snuggle against their mothers this way.

Today, in relation to sexuality, I am without inhibitions. I could tell you what took place in medical or psychological terminology, possibly scornfully or frivolously or boisterously, but, well, I just don't have anything more to say. It hurt. For days it even hurt to sit.

I was sleepy and tired. In the morning I marveled I had not figured out before that a man has to spread his legs. Now I know that he doesn't "have" to, that it is just a habit, but then I believed that everything I learned during that night was so and could not be any other way.

It seems I had, in those days, a very good appetite; as we woke up, pangs of hunger seized me. I threw on a lovely floor-length negligée that was given to me directly for this occasion, and I bounded home for some victuals. They greeted me with colossal consternation, "You! What are you doing here? Go right back, Erzsi will bring you something right away."

We were in a hurry to go into the city to register my new name and catch the express train to Budapest. János did not wait for me to get dressed, he went ahead.

When I got into the bathtub, the shower turned on unexpectedly and my hair became sopping wet. I dashed toward town but first ran into mother's to say good-bye. Again they

27

greeted me with consternation. Apparently, at such a time, the proper thing is to disappear, blushing, and I had no feeling for that, or for heaven knows what! They were also angry about my wet hair.

I could not buy a ticket on the bus because my purse was empty. (I received a thousand forints as a wedding present, but I did not want to touch that, intending it as a surprise; I gave it all to János, so I had already been without money for several days, and I was ashamed to ask my parents.)

Dealing with the ticket problem embarrassed me greatly, but the conductor smiled and said I should accept one as a gift from him; he had heard that yesterday was my wedding day. This made me very happy. But when I got off the bus, János gave me a tongue-lashing.

He was also angry about my hair, the suitcases, and about something else, I no longer remember what. His gray-green eyes darkened; his beard was very heavy, his face was dark blue even freshly shaven.

We traveled in first class to wonderful, distant Budapest. (That's funny, isn't it? But you don't know what Budapest and Hungary meant in Kolozsvár. Maybe you have some inkling of it by now.)

I don't remember a thing about the journey. In Budapest – I don't know at which station – I stood among the tracks, and suddenly my heart began to ache; it ached generally, and I became very sad.

Then the best man approached, the one who had flirted with me in the car on the way to the church, and he told me I looked beautiful, my traveling outfit was charming; he knew we were coming by train, but he did not want to *disturb* us. Then he made some innuendoes and kept complimenting me.

The Carlton. A suite overlooking the banks of the Danube. I was staying in a hotel for the first time in my life. When we dined in our rooms, a table was wheeled in, and a waiter stood there the whole time, changing the plates before us. The suite consisted of a bedroom and a living room. I do not remember anything else.

I was surprised I did not enjoy it more.

Air-raid sirens every night. One time, the whole building shook. A bomb had split the Ritz in two. The Carlton, too, is gone since then. The entire row of hotels was flattened by bombs.

We wandered about the city. Occasionally János left me alone. He had some conferences to attend, he said. I found this natural, though we were on our honeymoon.

I strolled along the banks of the Danube or I slept. I always wanted to sleep, I was inexpressibly tired and sleepy. This leads me to believe that we might have been together frequently at night, and, of course, there were the incessant air-raid alerts.

Then we went to Csákvár, Majk, and Eger. (Exactly ten years later, I was in the same hotel, in the same room with Miklós.)

In Eger we had a quarrel, and he left me standing on the street. On the very same day, I found out that he had given five hundred pengős to the college where he had studied, and had not told me about it. That he failed to mention it to me hurt me deeply. After all, I would have been very pleased about it. I gathered from a conversation I had with his cleric teacher that he had handed the money over the day before. He donated it out of my thousand forints. (In those days, that amounted to a half-year's salary.)

I have no memories of Eger other than this, just the city. We had planned that, on our way home, we would stop awhile in Budapest. We found out from the newspapers that they were establishing ghettos there. We did not want to believe they would do this, and if they actually did, even then not in Transylvania, that was impossible. But we immediately started for home.

We were the only Christians in our entire apartment house. The residents on the floor above us were very good friends; they were the ones who, right in the middle of a terrible housing shortage, turned over to us the ground-floor section of the building; they were drawing closer together because they were afraid. We served as a screen for them in matters of one kind or another; they helped János, who was then working for the Helikon Publishers, to a second job and income. He had also obtained his position at the Helikon through the intervention of our Jewish friends, particularly mine. Laci Kovács's wife, the bright and energetic Sulika who, the truth be told, actually ran the Helikon and the Szépmíves

Céh, another publishing house, was a Jew herself. So we rushed home.

The German occupation.

I am crossing the promenade at night on the way home. German tanks stand under the century-old wild chestnuts, ready to fire. Soldiers beside them, motionless and mute. Only their lighted cigarettes glow red in the darkness of the blackout and the foliage. It seems as if I can hear them breathing. A woman is walking alone in the darkness in front of the tanks, and the soldiers watch, motionless and silent. I am afraid. Not for myself, I do not count. It was strange how quiet it was, not a murmur, not a movement on the entire long road. This scene still haunts me. It was then I began to fear the Germans.

Terror and turmoil everywhere.

When we were being married, the Yellow Star already had to be worn. Böske Horváth, my girlfriend, did not come; she would not, she said, go to a Calvinist church, and I rebuked her stupidly, saying I willingly went to a synagogue with her. The young girl with whom my brother was in love, Margitka, did not come, either; but that did not surprise me, because I was friends with her only outside my home. Ferkó Dóry, when he learned he had to wear a star, suffered a crying fit and never left his apartment again.

Pista Kovács brought him to the wedding in a jacket in a taxi, saying he would tear apart anyone who dared to demand their papers. All this was a part of the atmosphere of the first days of my marriage, and it was with this memory that we hurried home from Budapest.

The day after we arrived home, they hauled off Imre Ká-dár[1] from our street. János ran to the school for his little girl, Anna, so she would not go home, and took her to Sulika. From there she was sent for safety to the provinces. She survived. In the meantime, Jánoska, their son, ran home and looked for Anna at our place. I detained him to no avail, he left. *He* did not survive. I have no other recollection of these days other than waiting with the Sebőks, who lived in the building, for the time when they would be taken away. It was horrible. Of course, we did not sit idly by. We succeeded in getting Péter, the Sebőks' son, into forced labor service. Soldiers had to be fitted out hastily, within hours. My sister

30

Irénke whipped the soldier's cap off her suitor's head, for which she was then put in jail. To this day I do not understand why she did it, for she was the only anti-Semite in the family. My brother Egon's hobnailed boots were a bit large for Péter; he returned them after the war with thanks.

Meanwhile, we ran about with suitcases, warm clothing, medicines, false papers, false medical certificates. We helped confine people in mental institutions, and so on. Others did the same; in those days, this was a matter of course.

János behaved very decently, not just with me, but with everyone. He helped without a word, he felt no fear, and he did not expect any expressions of gratitude. Other than that, he kept his silence. I was unaware of many things myself. The Gestapo took the most notable and wealthiest Jews into custody at night. My brother Egon was working for the city. The Germans always requested a truck from there. This way we knew about it in advance. I passed the tip on to Böske, she sent it on, and then they would not sleep in their own beds that night.

Böske and her family brought their jewels and other valuables over to our place. We rescued Ferkó Dőry, he became a soldier. They hauled away Margitka, Egon's sweetheart, in a garbage truck.

They were coming closer to our street. Sebők, his elderly mother, Mrs. Sebők, János and I spent the evenings talking endlessly. Then – well, they are not coming today, we can go to bed.

Mrs. Sebők lugged her belongings to our place in the daytime. The elderly mother suffered a stroke; half her side became paralyzed. Let's go quickly, get papers – we can save her from the camp! I sat on the bed beside her and assured her that she would not be taken away, that she would get to the hospital. When I ran off to the market, she wept and shouted, "Call her back, I believe her when she says I won't be hauled away."

Three days later, they hauled away all the residents in the building. They herded them down the staircase. There were little children, howling in despair; milk bottles broke, milk ran down the steps. I rushed out to help them. I wanted to speak to Magda. A gendarme yelled at me, "What do you want from them?" and he pushed me back in through the vestibule door. Magda, Mrs. Sebők, smiled and waved as she went down the stairs. The gendarme slammed the door in my face; I stood against the wall and heard the rattle in the old woman's breathing. Her son pleaded, "Don't rush her, the poor woman has had a stroke." "Then we will make her journey easier with a rifle butt," I heard this, too; then János grabbed my wrist, pushed me into the living room, and locked the door on me. This was his most compassionate act during the seven years of our marriage.

The two of us were alone in the entire building. My parents were away on their summer holiday. János spent the days in town. I cleaned the house, cooked, and waited for him to come home.

The building gave me the shivers, the bolted doors, the basement. I never went down when we had an air raid. I opened all the windows according to regulations. I sat down at my desk, which stood in the corner. I looked at my parent's place, directly across the street. My cat came over to me frequently. But one time János found it there, snatched it up, and threw it out the window. Our apartment was on the mezzanine; the cat landed in the rosebushes. I began crying and shouting. From that time on, the cat appeared only when it saw that János was not at home.

Meanwhile, life went on, of course. I had beautiful clothes. I had never had so many clothes before. (As a child and a young girl, I wore hand-me-down, poorly altered clothes.) Parties, theatre, hustle and bustle.

János gave me a beautiful Alsatian; it made me very happy. But then some Germans stole it. I licked my home like a mother pussycat.

Márta Prámer,[2] that spiteful beast, said at the end of the war, "Do you know what I really regret? That they also destroyed your beautiful home."

János lived in one room. It contained many books, Biedermeier parlor furniture, a desk, a couch, and an antique wardrobe.

I furnished my room with its corner windows very charmingly, harmoniously, cozily with antique furniture that I very fondly collected piece by piece. (Today I do not understand where I got the taste and energy, given my state of mind at the time.)

A small modern dining room looked out upon a most pleasant and very usable balcony covered with flowers. The kitchen was a typical provincial kitchen with a cleanly scrubbed floor and a splendid stove; it was my pride and joy. I canned preserves and gave dinners; I set the table decoratively and cooked very well; and I tried to dress fashionably, in accordance with János's wishes.

He wanted me to use makeup. This is one thing I did not do, because I did not know how. (This is true. Today, women are born with this skill, we had to learn it.) Besides, it would have been absurd. I was rosy-cheeked, my lips were still ruby-red. My hair was naturally wavy and I hardly ever went to a hairdresser.

I don't remember whether János and I ever discussed intellectual or other problems. He did not like it if I talked about my feelings. He was extremely taciturn and sullen. He was marked by some kind of strange coldness and impassivity. He found it difficult to form human relationships. He had completely lost interest in everything; after three and a half years at the front, he knew – and somewhat cynically expected – that the Russians would come inevitably, that we would lose the war, and he also knew a few things about life in the Soviet paradise.

He wanted and would have liked to write, but he wrote very rarely and very little. He never finished anything. And he drank. He drank heavily and regularly. It did not show on him; I never saw him drunk, rarely even tipsy. Several times daily he would drink one or two shots of hard liquor, and wine and wine-and-soda alternately. After a checkup, the doctor informed him that he had a chronic liver condition and must stop drinking because it will finish him off.[3] He did not care and did not undergo treatment.

We fought furiously over this. Love, pleas, logical persuasion, medical and other arguments did not affect him; he just shrugged his shoulders and went on drinking. I changed my tactics. When he took a drink, I always drank twice the amount. Until then, I had drunk casually and willingly and became tipsy quickly. Now I was often drunk; I became sick. I began to hate wine.

He backed down a little, then resumed drinking; the condition of his liver worsened. I fell into despair. I played my last card; when he drank, no matter how little, I promptly drank myself senseless.

This played out roughly like this: We went into town upon an invitation to dinner. Without saying a word, János turned into a restaurant. By now I no longer pleaded with him not to drink; doing that would generate an unbearable tension that lasted for days. He ordered the one deciliter of hard liquor for himself, a beer for me. I could not change the order; he abhorred all scenes in front of waiters and any strangers. I didn't, it made no difference to me; I knew this and never spoke up. I stood up after a time, I had to go out. He took my purse without a word. I did not give a damn even about this. I went to the bar in a roundabout way and asked for a four-deciliter cognac. Somewhat amazed, the bartender asked, "How do you want it?" "In a glass," I answered politely. I drank it up with slow, uniform sips. (The smell of cognac even today sends a chill along the length of my spine.) "My husband will pay for it," I said casually, and I went back to the table. I don't know how four deciliters of cognac before dinner affects others, but it was way too much for me. But I held out until I fell full length. This in itself would have been cause enough for gossip, but the fact that my heart, or something, cannot tolerate alcohol just made things worse. Doctor, injections, commotion!

Perhaps, when I lay in a cold sweat with livid fingernails and lips, he was shaken, and embraced and kissed me. This was why he gave up drinking, or he had a feeling that I would stubbornly keep on doing it until I ran into serious trouble; I don't know why, but he did stop drinking. He was even willing to go on a diet.

Sometimes we amused ourselves. He enjoyed watching me when I was bathing, dressing, or undressing. I threw up barricades; he stole the keys, so I could not lock the doors. I enjoyed the fuss and the tussles enormously, but to undress naked in front of him – that really embarrassed me.

We made plans. He took over the periodical named *Pásztortűz*. We were determined to turn it into a serious publication. I helped him eagerly, I was at his beck-and-call. I wheedled my father out of his old office for the editorial staff, and painted and furnished it, even though I previously spent some time in the hospital, then had my tonsils removed, so that my heart would better withstand my overactive thyroid. But the sign on the door made me indefatigable, "Pásztortűz. Editorial Office of the Illustrated Monthly."

I believe that even though I went to bed with him readily, I surrendered myself reluctantly to his embraces. Whether this showed, I do not know. It is certain that I always accepted his advances. If I did not feel anything, that was good; I remained composed. But if I gave myself over to his embraces, I lay there, after a few moments, with my nerves stretched to the snapping point; the blood vessels throbbed in my head, and my heart would not subside. I did not want to disturb him by moving, because it made him angry; I was able to lie motionless beside him by producing a tonal muscular tension throughout my entire body, and when I could no longer endure this stretching, I relaxed, then stretched again and relaxed again. For this reason, I was afraid to let myself go completely, because when I lay there unsatisfied, I was miserable.

It was the middle of summer, and the Szépmíves Céh was sending János to the Book Fair in Budapest. He did not want to take me along, but I really wanted to go. Besides, because of the bombings of Budapest, I was afraid to let him be alone. I once happened to be at Helikon, and during a conversation, I heard Sulika say that Laci Kovács, her husband, never went to a book fair without her. What is more, it came out that my hotel bill would be covered; after all, I would be selling books at the pavilion. The fact that he did not want to take me with him hurt me terribly; we had been married only three months, but I just thought the reason could be something he did not want to talk to me about.

Then he suggested that I follow him two days later with my father, because it was too late to obtain a sleeping car ticket for me. That I, a young wife, should travel with my father and not my husband was so humiliating that I was ashamed to mention it at home. I replied that it would be a simpler solution for me if Pista Kovács accompanied me to Budapest, for he was willing to adjust his departure to mine.

Pista was a good friend of mine from my childhood, in a pleasant, good-natured, comradely relationship, open toward me but also to the outside world. He never burdened me with his love, which he quickly forgot; then he fell in love with Ricuka after Irénke and married her. I requited him with a friendship that lasted a lifetime. A sleeping car ticket instantly appeared, but I do not think this episode can somehow be forgotten.

A grand life went on in the pavilion in Budapest. I was a great favorite. Nyírő[5] related to everyone how I had been his daughter's classmate and the silly nonsense we whispered to each other at examinations. I told István Nagy[6] that my entire class was in love with him. Of course, then came Tamási, János Kemény, and old Miklós Bánffy[7] with his magnificent head and courtly manner. (Later Egon helped him to emigrate from Transylvania to Budapest, where he died very shortly thereafter.) I don't know how János took my triumphs. He once spoke to me coldly and bitingly, "Straighten your hat, you look like a clown!" This put a damper on my spirits for hours. We glowed and were happy for the last time. In the reannexed Transylvanian book pavilion, I was the Transylvanian woman being celebrated heartily and cordially. He was the poet, a member of the Transylvanian Helikon and Szépmíves Céh. We were the bearers of books by Transylvanian writers.

He frequently went his separate way; sometimes he gave a laconic account of where he had been.

Kolozsvár had been carpet-bombed. We wanted to return immediately, but it was not possible – the entire railway line had been bombed, no trains were running. No telegram or telephone connections were available. We could not even get any news through the ministry. How are my parents, my friends? What has become of the city? What has happened to the ghetto?

Finally we were able set out. At Szolnok, as I lowered the train window, a nauseating, strong odor swept in. It was the stench of burned corpses.

Later – I no longer remember which station it was – cattle cars with barbwire-covered windows stood parallel to us. Jews were being transported from Transylvania. They begged for food. We handed them whatever we could instantly find. (Mami, János's mother, had packed from rich Transdanubia, from the Esterházy manor house, for our journey.)

Rough shouting exploded, that of gendarmes and possibly of soldiers, too, "Who did that? You are not permitted to go near the locked box cars." They boarded our car to find the culprit. Since armed soldiers were patrolling between the two trains, they by and large took measure of the distance between cars. János, referring to his honor as an officer, protested and resented that they would suspect me and hold me responsible. "They will detach the car, they will not let the train leave until they capture the culprit." Finally an air raid came, and they had to release the train. I stood at the window; a young woman from Kolozsvár recognized me. She pressed her face against the barbwire and shouted to me, "See you again!" "Right! In the hereafter!" a gendarme yelled at her. I knew János shared my feelings. I anticipated Kolozsvár with growing anxiety; combined, this was way too much for me, but I saw he did not want me to speak. I kept silent. He did not speak about anything, either, not a single word.

Kolozsvár at last. The station was completely unscathed; its environs were completely demolished. They had bombed the environs of the railroad. A couple hundred dead, we were told. The newspapers admitted to just a few. The ghetto was hit. Egon went into the casualties area to meet Margitka and sneak a package to her. She had lost everything. Irén and I selected underwear and warm clothing from our things, my mother prepared some food. In 1988, in Kiriat Tiron, Margitka, now bearing the name of Miriam, related this to us in the following words: "Egon gathered the dead together, and I kept running alongside him (I did not even reach his shoulder, I was so little), asking him, 'Why? Why? Why?' He did not say a word, he did not look at me. His tears flowed continuously."

Everyone in the family was unhurt. I thought this was the most difficult day of my life. (Dear God, how mistaken I was!)

Transylvania was declared a theatre of war. But we went about our lives. You, too, will remember how, theatre of war or not, life bubbled merrily. Theatres and movie houses were packed; it was impossible to find an empty table in restaurants; outings and the entertainment of guests at home followed one another in quick succession. That was when Zoli Jékely's piece entitled *Angelit and the Hermits*[8] had its premiere. His wife, Adrienne Jancsó, played the leading role. It was, of course, a great event.

Then Páger came down from Budapest with Marci Kerecsendi Kiss to direct *The First.*[9] Marci was János's classmate. A political tension existed between us, but we all tried to paper it over; we avoided sensitive topics as much as possible. We were once sitting on the terrace of the New York Café; the topic of conversation was Tamási's divorcing Magdó. "Why, of course," Páger said. "She is a Jew." "She was a Jew when he married her," I retorted. (Tamási[10] put off the divorce until after the war; he even rescued Magda and her family.) I mean to say, skirmishes did occur, but I participated in them only very rarely and marginally. János did not like me to speak up in company, and it was impossible for me to discuss anything with him, either. My conduct came up for discussion only if it displeased him. No matter what I expressed, he remarked on it only when he objected to it. Even then, he offered no comment, just this: Don't talk politics, you don't understand it. Or: It would be better if you kept your mouth shut when you want to say stupid things.

My natural openness and lack of inhibitions began to fade slowly. Even today I cannot dance loosely and easily because he pointed out to me, scoffing, sneering, that possibly I should not dance, because I move like an elephant. (Yet how I enjoyed and still enjoy dancing.)

Since I loved János, and his opinion mattered to me, he shook my self-confidence very easily and quickly. Somehow I still could put up with this, but I found his coldness and sternness unbearable. After all, I had a loving nature. At home I was my father's and mother's darling and my siblings' intimate friend; the servants, the dog, the cat – they all loved me. Add my friends to them. Miklós, you remember that when we were in Transylvania for the first time in ten years, with what love Böske Horváth showered me, and that when we wanted to board the train to return home, Pista Kovács was waiting at the train at midnight. He and Böske went to the train three nights, because they did not know when we were leaving and wanted to say good-bye one more time.

Lonci was my friend since we were in kindergarten together. Berta Biró wrote me to go to her immediately when, after four months of marriage, her husband died in her arms, and she was left pregnant. (The son she was carrying then asked me recently how was the "gentleman" who wrote *The Youth of Szeben*[11] because he had read about him in the newspaper.) Love and trust surrounded me like a mother's warm embrace. Only János did not love me. I could not get used to that. But I could not complain to anyone. Not even to Berta who turned to me in her greatest crisis and whom I continue to love deeply to this day.

For seven years I never spoke to anyone about my marriage and my problems. Even today I can only try to guess why. At the time I did not think about them; maybe I did not even notice them. Last summer I became more aware of them when Auntie Róza, my mother's only woman friend and cousin, told me that my mother once lamented to her that she felt I was unhappy but I was not saying anything either to my family or to my closest girlfriends.

Once a small pimple appeared on my inner labium. I was uneasy for days; I finally mentioned it to János, very ashamed. He immediately turned very gloomy and promptly sent me to the doctor. It was diagnosed as gonorrhea. (Today, many are, I know, uninformed about this disease; unfortunately, I am not. It is a venereal disease, but it is not syphilis.)

At the time we still had our beautiful Alsatian, Fritz. At nine months, he was as big as a calf. János did not go to the doctor with me; I took Fritz along. I do not know why, but I think I was apprehensive. The doctor had a tiny, white Pekingese. This wild beast Fritz, who attacked man and animal if he was not restrained, stopped in front of this puny, miserable white ball and quivered; he was afraid and did not budge; he let the Pekingese attack his legs viciously. The doctor and I were both astounded.

How does it feel to lie on the examining table with thighs spread to let someone reach in and look inside you when you are nineteen (you get used to it in time) and to answer embarrassing questions so you can be told you have a venereal disease?

I cannot put it down in writing. Maybe a man cannot even imagine it.

Oh well, I did not say anything. Then the doctor said, "This is not the typical form in which the disease manifests itself. The skin here is still young and overly sensitive, as is the case with every young girl. Moreover, it is my duty to advise you that this is grounds for divorce. I have recorded it in my journal, and I am ready whenever you wish to issue the official confirmation. The court accepts it in every case." "Why should I get a divorce?" I asked in amazement. "Because your husband picked this up somewhere." "But what if I was the one who got it?" "Yes, if you are living with several men at the same time, then this is not really a cause for divorce now, is it?" he said, seemingly greatly amused by what he had said.

Then, probably from the idiotic look on my face, he realized it was not that which I had in mind, and he stated that something like this can be caught only by contact. "Maybe from the toilet seat," I said. At which he jokingly said, "Possibly, but it is highly uncomfortable." I did not understand him. He must have felt sorry for me, because he talked to me at great length. "Young lady, you are even younger and more innocent than your actual years. Where did you get such naiveté and trust from? Apparently you have fallen into the hands of a scoundrel, because nobody else could have done this to you. Take my word, accept the certificate, and institute divorce proceedings; if you do not, you will pay dearly for this marriage."

I became so indignant at this that I did not say a single word in reply. I paid and left. I went to another doctor for treatment, so I would never see him again.

I understood the toilet-seat innuendo while on the way home. I was completely alone on the darkening promenade, but I blushed and ran home the length of Rákóczi Road. Then I began to grow suspicious; yet, in a curious way, it was not the facts that hurt but how much the both of us were at the mercy of a third party, the doctor. At home, I told János in a few words what had taken place; then I took hold of his head, turned his face toward mine, so we could both look straight into each other's eyes, and I implored him, "I am not mad at you, but in God's name, tell me the truth. Did you catch it from someone else? If you lie to me now, I won't be able to bear it." (I only have to close my eyes to see his look, his eyes.) He had beautiful greenish gray eyes and a high forehead; he looked

very sincere and said somehow with strength from within –
but, of course, you have to look with such great sincerity and
shock when you are lying; when horribly embarrassed, you
can do nothing other than muster all your strength. "How
silly are! Of course I did not bring it home from someone else.
Remember, you yourself complained how you lost your bal-
ance and flopped onto the public toilet at Kolozsvár, and had
to wash yourself afterwards. That is when you must have
got it."

Later, I tried to find an excuse for him, that the lie was
justified from his viewpoint, but to no avail. This is what I
felt to be his true and indelible betrayal: his look. (What is
the wound that cannot be healed? Well, to me it is that sincere look. I can forgive, indeed forget, every deception, boor-
ishness, betrayal, anything. Which is no reason, of course,
to take advantage of it. But when offering everything, when
I meet everything head on and ask only for sincerity – it's
like some form of mental disorder – I want the truth, I am
unable to forgive a lie.) A few days later, signs of the disease
also broke out on him. I plunged into despair, thinking I had
infected him. Painful days and weeks followed. I won't go
into details. He recovered quickly; men do not have the sensitive structure that supports childbirth and is so entirely
exposed to disease. I could not receive treatment by injection, which generates a fever, because of my heart. It wasn't
even a drop in the bucket for him; he recovered. Naturally
we did not have any intercourse; we did not feel like it.

My mother had left for Auntie Rózsika's in Kecskemét to rest
after her thrombosis, but she was no longer able to return
because Transylvania was sealed off; we really became a theatre of war. One morning, we woke up to the sound of heavy
cannon fire; we observed the muzzle fire on Feleki Peak. In
short, Rumania left the coalition on August 23.

And it did so in its own fashion. The chief staff officers or
the leaders of the nation invited the German chief officers to
a champagne dinner. They got them drunk, then murdered
and hacked them into pieces. In the chaos, they routed the
rank-and-file, captured them, and upon their surrender, gave
them their orders and they "deserted," thus leaving the coali-

tion.[12] How painstaking and clumsy Hungary was with its badly disguised, badly organized attempts at withdrawal!

Rumanian artillery, a Rumanian army stood on Feleki Peak. At their feet was Kolozsvár, full of Germans. Airplanes patrolled above us; sometimes they strafed the streets with their machine guns. I looked at the traces of bullets lodged in the asphalt at the head of Ferenc Deák Street.

So, Rumania allied itself with the Soviet Union on August 24, 1944, and the front-line stretched to the mountain peaks above Kolozsvár. The Germans applied their usual, tested tactics: with respect to Rumania, now declared an enemy, they allowed Hungarian armed forces to occupy the territory and annex it to the motherland. (An inspiration of Lucifer's, wasn't it?) They recaptured Torda in twenty-four hours at the cost of horrible casualties. We observed the gunfire of this battle on Feleki Peak. With this tactic they poured fresh fuel on Rumanian and Hungarian hatred; the Rumanians came raging to re-occupy Kolozsvár. It would be the only excuse, later on, for the arrival of the Soviet army there.

Long before the Rumanian attack, the Esterházys[13] wrote to my family, advising them to send me to Csákvár ahead of the Russians. My mother-in-law was serving as their head housekeeper. At the time, their manor house was already under the protection of the Swiss Red Cross. "Here in Transdanubia there will not be any warfare, English occupation, and so on." I will be completely safe. My family and János made desperate efforts to get me to go, but I resisted stubbornly. (We really did know we had to lose the war, but even we did not imagine that defeat would be burdened by a spiteful and triumphant Rumania.) I did not want to leave while my family and János were in Transylvania. Suddenly it seemed that we were caught in a rat trap in Kolozsvár. It was a major question as to whether the Germans wanted to hold on to the city or to abandon it. Obviously, it was indefensible militarily, but what did it matter to the Germans that a city was to be shelled to bits to gain them a few hours' delay.

We went along the streets. Giant posters. "I order the material and personal evacuation of the city. Signed, Lajos

Veress,[14] Commander of the Rumanian Army Corps." And a terse sentence, "Escape trains departing." Who has to leave the city? Inhabitants, or soldiers? If soldiers, then why the posters? If inhabitants, then what does "material evacuation" mean?

We did not reflect for long; airplanes pounded the street with machine guns from one end to the other wherever people gathered.

A dreadful afternoon. I was glad I had not left, and I awaited the future with a strange, breath-constricting anxiety.

The family – father, Egon, Irénke, János – decided we should go, we must escape. I too wanted that; I guarded János jealously. He did not know a single word of Rumanian; he had come from the motherland. We had a concern with and a right to Transylvania in one way or another. But I did not want the Rumanians to find him there.

On the day of our flight Böske Horváth came out to our place: we had hidden her belongings. She asked us to stay. She had Rumanian and Communist friends, she would protect us. I did not want to. Now *she* took one or two of my things with her to take care of for me.

My father and Egon scolded me for not leaving sooner. Now, what will they do with me? János said, "I should have been more firm. But drop it, it doesn't make any difference now."

Egon obtained a German truck for two paintings, some food, gasoline, and gold. "It is coming for us at midnight."

We began to pack feverishly, everything valuable in large cases. Even bedclothes and pictures. Then we sat and waited. The family prepared comforters and big pillows for me to lie on in the truck. (I still had not recovered completely.)

At two in the morning, a smaller vehicle arrived. Repacking. One packing case per family, four suitcases per person.

We repacked and waited.

Day broke. The truck did not come. As I opened the cases on this slowly breaking dawn, I rearranged the apartment exactly as it had been. I even put back in their places the pictures, the tablecloths, the vases, as if nothing had happened, as if I were not preparing to leave and abandon my home forever to whoever would come and occupy it.

I turned on the lights behind the lowered shutters and surveyed all the rooms. Everything was in order, the kitchen, too. I washed the demitasse cups and put them in their place. (The suitcases were standing outside the door. They contained mostly personal belongings.)

At seven o'clock in the morning, Egon entered, sweating and desperate: This truck was not coming, either. He had got hold of a pushcart.

Repacking and loading up in less than thirty minutes all it could carry from the possessions of two apartments and five persons and pushing it ahead of us, we set off for the station to plead to be taken aboard the train for refugees. (I could discard only wrapped things; as I tossed them away, a box of photographs broke apart and pictures flew in different directions onto the floor, the table, and the sofa; the sun shone in powerfully.) Throughout, János did not say much. He was surly and withdrawn. He did not interfere with the packing. He didn't even help.

A terrible pandemonium reigned at the railroad station. Army trucks passed by its front ceaselessly. The refugee train was nowhere in sight. We unloaded our possessions in one of the waiting rooms amid shattered glass and debris.

My father said he was hungry, he'd seen some fruit in one of the shops, he will locate it, and he headed back to the city.

Egon and Irénke hunted for some kind of suitable motor vehicle and took their possessions with them on the pushcart, so they could stake out a place immediately and then come back for us. I stood guard over our belongings. János started off to the left, in the direction of the garrison headquarters.

Suddenly a horrible shouting broke out; everybody scurried and fled. An old railway man stood on the platform pointing to the sky, "Bombers!" Then his face turned pale, "Look, there come the bombers!" Three formations of what looked like three specks were descending above the buildings. I ran toward garrison headquarters. I found János there; we ran, holding hands, to an emergency air-raid shelter. It was a sort of corridor for an underground bunker; we had to climb down an iron ladder into the shaft. People pushed and pulled each other frantically. At the moment a plane flew directly above us. I stood to the side, spellbound. I was astounded that a formation of three specks was diving directly at our heads. Somebody howled like an animal, "We are done for!"

There was no time to climb down. János grabbed me, picked me up, and threw me into the shaft, then jumped in after me. By this time, bombs were exploding outside. I fell on people, my wrist became wedged in a crack in the wall. Actually, and in every sense of the word, János saved my life, because I did not even try to move. In a strange way I never felt grateful to him. I was amazed, however, at his presence of mind.

We stood leaning against the wall in this narrow concrete corridor, many of us. A great faintness overcame me; I did not dare turn my head to the side to look at those who had remained outside and were now being brought down, horribly torn to shreds, but still alive. One kept trying to say something but could not speak. He articulated something time and again with an unintelligible rattling in his throat. They closed the concrete cover of the shaft. The bomb hits could be heard, the bomb hits, every one of them close. At times the ground shook around us. A railroad man stood at the extension phone, signaled for silence, and said, "We have casualties. Send first aid!" The same thing ten times over. Then, "I understand." A long pause, he is paying attention. He wipes his brow, "They cannot help us."

Then he goes to some device to start the air circulation. It fails to function. He struggles with it; others come to his aid, but the device does not work. The concrete lid that covers the ladder to the shaft has to be opened because the air is being used up rapidly. We will suffocate. The railroad men say, "This is the service shelter, the air-raid shelter; civilians and soldiers must get out, we cannot leave our stations, we cannot run off. A few of you must climb out between bombings and run to the buildings across the street."

Wild squabbling, "Don't you have any humanity?" "Do understand, there is no air, we will all choke to death here."

An officer takes out his revolver, raises it, ready to fire, "Soldiers! The first group get moving!" The railroad man beside the telephone, "The rescue train has been hit! The qualified, the stretcher bearers get going!" Without thinking I step forward. János pulls me back, "What are you doing?" "I am

45

a trained nurse," I reply. At that, he restrains and holds me tightly, "Nobody here knows that." "But I do," I answer, at which he covers my mouth. The first group starts off. They climb up the ladder. The concrete lid cannot be removed. We are buried alive. What will become of us?

Others fiddle with the pump; meanwhile, the railroad man telephones, "There is no air! There is no air! We are buried, send help, send help!" Then he issues orders, "Don't talk! Don't move! That way we use less air. Let's all breathe even, shallow!"

We stand in silence, like sardines; we sweat and breathe desperately because there is still some air. (If I take a deeper breath now, then maybe I will be able to bear it longer.) The telephone was the most frightful. In the deadly, sweaty silence, only the sound of the rattles issuing from the throats of the injured could be heard. "There are seventy of us, we can last only ten to fifteen minutes longer." Then, "The telephone is not working." He lowered his arm together with the receiver.

I leaned toward János's face (he was holding me in an embrace), "I don't want to die." He replied with a significant smile, "The others don't, either."

Somehow this lessened my concern. "Maybe a bomb will strike here and squash this bird cage." By the time I said this, I shuddered: I could feel the shattered walls falling on me. János noticed, because he whispered, "I will lean over you. Don't be afraid, only I can fall on you." Somebody shouted at us to stop talking. The terror of the previous minutes continued. We waited... Then I began choking, then everything turned black.

When I opened my eyes, I saw a black aperture, a palm-sized aperture in front of my face with little green plates revolving in it, like the tuning eye of a radio. Air came slowly seeping in. I was being held up to the height of the low ceiling, so I could get some air directly, in front of a vent of the air pump, which had somehow started up. (I had lost consciousness so quickly because the tuberculosis from which I had suffered had reduced my lung capacity.)

But enough about this day. We were under fire in this concrete corridor from nine in the morning until six in the evening. When they somehow opened the concrete lid, every time

46

we crawled out, after two steps, back we went. And more horrors occurred, but I do not want to go on relating them in
detail. Like cattle, like dumb animals, we did not have an
inkling, in this concrete hole, that only the railway station
was under fire in the entire city. The escape train was also
shot up; the wounded and the dead lay alongside the tracks.
János behaved nobly throughout it all, in the true sense of
the word.

We got away toward dark. We located our luggage in the
ruins. The others were nowhere to be found. Away quickly,
away from here; let's not have to crawl back there again.

It was not possible to go back to the city; we were told that
Szamos Bridge had been blown up. We found a drunken carriage driver who did not know where to go or what to do with
himself. For a large sum of money he accepted the terms that
we would go with him wherever his horse took him. Quickly,
up with the luggage.

The frightened, scrawny horse started off at a gallop. We
soon reached the highway in the direction of Szucság. There
he dropped us off and, walking, he led his horse into the
fields. We hid under the bushes of an embankment because
planes attacked the road frequently. This was the direction
in which the military was retreating.

We waved our arms in vain; not a single vehicle stopped.
Then I said to János, "Just hide in the bushes; they will
stop for a lone woman, and then they won't say they won't
pick you up." Angrily but without a word, he slipped into
the bushes. (I respected him for that very much; he handled
it without getting on his high horse; he did not start strut-
ting around like a rooster.)

The first military truck stopped, and every one thereafter. But not one of them took as aboard. "We can't, we
can't. There's no room; it's a truck, it's not fit for a woman."
Half-empty personnel carriers did not pick us up, either.
I grew very desperate. I hung on to the side of the next vehicle and pleaded, "Don't you have any heart? Don't you have
a mother? A sister?"

The driver suddenly leaned out of the vehicle. "We can't
pick up anyone, it's an order. Don't waste your time. Escape

as best you can. I say this because I do have a mother and a sister."

I went and hid with János in the bushes. "Do you understand this? They can't pick up refugees. What is going on?" "Bureaucracy," he said, then when he saw I didn't understand what he was alluding to, "The military, orders, orders! There is no point fretting about it, everything must be accepted as it comes... nothing can be done about it."

I was very worked up, and I really would have loved to look right into the eyes of Lajos Veress,[15] the commander of the Transylvanian army corps, and ask him how he could be so cruel. What could he possibly say? He issues the order to flee, then does not allow us to escape. (I had no idea that on one occasion I would converse with him for hours, and tell him I understood this order of his and respected him for it as well as other things. Five years later, he was condemned to death because of the first Communist conspiracy, but, as I remember, he was pardoned.)

The first German truck I hailed stopped to pick us up. It was a truck with exceptionally high sides. We were unable to climb up, but a Hungarian vehicle coming behind it stopped immediately; they flung János up somehow and then handed me up to him, then the luggage, very quickly. We were instantly on our way, for the road was under attack.

A small package remained behind; it contained two kilos of coffee, one kilo of tea, and a gold cigarette case. One of the Hungarian infantrymen ran after our truck; taking a full swing, he hurled it after us. We could not catch it. He picked it up from the ground, and running at breakneck speed, he threw it again with all his might. It fell to the ground. I leaned out, and cupping my hand, I shouted to him, "It's yours, enjoy it!" This was my first moment of abandon, and I thought, how nice, poetic justice – that life can, after all, be good, for destiny repaid this soldier's warm and devoted help by having this package remain behind. No matter how hard he tried, it stayed in his hands. (Do any of you today know what so much coffee and tea meant back then?) "How surprised he will be when he discovers the gold cigarette case," I laughed at János. He knit his brows, looked at me thoughtfully, and said coldly and sharply, "He'll be as happy as a blind horse with half an eye." The truck took us to Nagykároly.

They dropped us off at the side of the road. I sat on the suitcases on the road; János began looking for a place where we could rest a bit. People surrounded us and stared at us, "Look, refugees." They knew nothing about Kolozsvár and the front. We reached Debrecen in a couple of days by means of military vehicles. Finally, we were in the longed-for, the trustworthy motherland where there is only one enemy, or rather two, not three, as back home.

We were pretty shabbily welcomed in Debrecen. The townspeople had survived a heavy air attack the day before. They were furious and afraid. I had not experienced anything like it anywhere.

No one wanted to take us in, even though we were exhausted to death by now. In his rage, János would not speak, even to me. "Then *I* will do it," I said. I went into a house and begged our way in with great difficulty. They let us in and provided a bare sofa for us. (There were only bare pieces of furniture in the house. Were they storing everything in the cellar?) They sat there themselves. We tumbled onto the sofa without taking our clothes off and fell asleep. Then they woke us up, "Air-raid alert, come with us." Fine, but not until the planes come.

I was barely alive from exhaustion. No, they are responsible, we have to go down right now. The wretches! But they did not give me a place to sit. I was unable to stand, I told them. I told them I was going to the toilet, and I stretched out in the grass in front of the air-raid shelter and fell asleep. They shook me awake in the morning and cursed me within earshot, saying how rebellious these Transylvanians are. (An alert is not the same as an attack; why shouldn't I be able to sleep in front of the shelter?) János didn't utter a word. He stole a pair of goggles from them; the dust and wind in the open trucks had done my eyes in badly. The corneas were red, swollen, and inflamed. We left Debrecen during an air-raid alert. Again it was the Germans who gave us a lift. The trailer was a mammoth petrol tank; János sat on it. It was an uncomfortable and smelly place. It wasn't possible to hang on to the top of the cylinder. It was for this reason that a German soldier took me off and seated me next to him on the driver's seat. We couldn't converse. Low-flying planes swooshed –

the hell they swooshed, they zoomed and stormed like the wind above us – and took us under fire.

To my greatest shock, we didn't stop and run for our lives; we didn't even accelerate to top speed, but continued to jog along at a very reduced, even tempo-the entire line of trucks. (I really must ask a soldier what purpose this serves...)[16] This German couldn't answer any question posed in Hungarian; he just shrugged his shoulders and kept his eyes glued to the road. So intense a fear seized me that I felt like screaming or praying aloud. – Not as I had in the bunker, that was different. The thought of János sitting atop the petrol tank alone when he might be killed was driving me crazy.

I didn't move or speak, but I swore that if we escaped with our lives, I would never tell a lie again, I would not acquire anything for myself, I would never wear silk stockings. (Today I can only laugh at this or feel pity for myself at how little I had to pledge from my meager life.)

Then a hit behind us, a hit to the side, "Dear God, if you have any mercy in you, grant that the bomb should land here and not on the trailer. If it falls here, I renounce everything; I will lead the life of an ascetic to the end of all my born days." Well, something like this.

In my great anxiety, it never occurred to me that if I summon death, I cannot make any pledges on my life. Nor could I think through the notion that if the gasoline truck behind us exploded, we would also be blown sky-high – no need for pledges. If we got the direct hit I prayed for, János would not escape atop the benzene tank, either.

Well, no matter, a human being sometimes walks on the edge of insanity. Be that as it may, I arrived at a conclusion: I would never again sit apart from him in a vehicle. (We then quarreled a lot over this.) This is how you are, if you love someone deeply.)

Am I talking too much about the air raids? Even today my stomach and intestines churn a little at the drone of an airplane. To me, the thought is reassuring, and it dissipates my fear, if I know that the atom bomb will be released at a great height and fall silently. And if then the roof, the house, the concrete will not bury anyone, there will be no detonation, no throat rattle, no death cry, and our limbs will disintegrate in silence... We will turn into dust. It is only to be hoped for.

A REFUGEE'S IDYLL

We arrived in Budapest in September at the end of an air attack. The Shell Oil refineries were ablaze; we were traveling in their vicinity. The city, the streets, everything was black with smoke.

Life in the city was in full swing. People ran to the air-raid shelters, laughing and joking. They danced as they cleaned up the ruins. Restaurants were jammed. Something sinewy, suitable for chewing, or a vegetable was served in the place of regular fare, but the waiters served it politely and cheerfully. What a tempered city this Budapest is! (I had occasion to admire it later on as well.) We found a place for ourselves at the Esterházy Palace on Castle Hill. Cleanliness, quiet, tranquility. If we descended to ever deeper and deeper levels in the system of cellars under Castle Hill, we could walk through the labyrinth on stairs and in passageways, and not hear the din of bombardments. It was as if we had wound up in an enchanted realm. The cellars were clean, properly tended, well-ventilated even at the depth of three levels, and fresh wells were available.

It was here I saw a geyser gas water heater in a bathroom for the first time. (I was afraid of it.) During our flight, wind and dust had so dishevelled my hair, I was barely able to comb it out when it was wet; I had to cut off some of it.

I went down to the South Railway Station to inquire about a train.

An air alert. I was so afraid of being caught in the railroad area that I tore across the Vérmező and up the stairs of Castle Hill. You were not permitted to stay out on the streets during an alert. Nobody was around to take note, only some German soldiers lying on their stomachs in the grass on a slope of the Vérmező (still a deep, grassy basin back then). They shouted at me to run into some building. Weren't they permitted to? Or were there too many of them? They stayed put. Always disciplined, always silent.

Then Bicske. We were heading for Csákvár, and we stayed with Marci Kerecsendi Kiss and her family. It was then we learned that Kolozsvár had fallen a few hours after our departure. Nothing else. Not a bit of additional news came until spring.

János called up the Csákvár forestry office and asked them to inform his mother that we were alive and on our way. He stood beside a desk and made the call. I lay on a sofa and watched him.

Marci and his mother were also in the room. We were quiet, so we would not disturb him. Finally he got through. Then he said, "This is so and so speaking. Forestry Counselor, please inform my mother I have arrived safe and sound; I am here in Bicske and will start for home tomorrow." Then to a question at the other end of the line, he replied woodenly, "She is here, too." That unknown man, who had never seen me, found it odd that János used the first person singular; evidently, that was why he inquired if I was with him.

At first, such a strange sense of shame seized me at the possibility that Marci and his mother would also guess what was going on that my heart skipped a beat.

Suddenly this became completely inconsequential to me, and those moments came to my mind when I had prayed for his life: for the bomb to fall on me and not him.

Then it struck me that I had left Transylvania, and I was now in another, an unfamiliar world. I lost my footing. I had to pay heed to the fact that I was completely alone amid every horror. I wanted to flee to the deadly minutes in the bunker; I was hanging on to the fact that then we were together.

Mami, János's mother, was the head housekeeper at the Esterházy manor house in Csákvár. The year before, when I went there to introduce myself to Mami, Monika Esterházy and I became friends, and I was also a guest at the manor house in Majk. (Monika was a strange creature, as was the entire family; but more about this later.) We were now going to Mami's; it was the natural thing to do.

Mami was a short, buxom creature (how could she have given birth to such a tall son?) with childlike blue eyes, a loose German chignon; her chignon looked like a braided brioche; she never used face powder or cologne in her life. She had come from Vienna some time ago, but she still spoke in Hungarian a little uncomfortably, with an accent. The elderly mistress of Csákvár didn't know any Hungarian at all; perhaps, that was why they engaged Mami as head housekeeper of the manor house after the death of her husband.

Mami was the most decent person I ever met in my life. She was a bit deaf to ideas, so was her hearing. Her spirit was not deaf. But it was very difficult to communicate with her in everyday life. János spoke in a very low voice to begin with. If I tried to act as her interpreter by raising my voice, she was annoyed and gestured impatiently for me to desist. She did not understand at all the more complicated Hungarian words, the looser locutions, the allusions, nor the war, either. She had only the faintest ideas about Transylvania, and she had never spoken with anyone who had experienced an air raid.

Csákvár was actually a village. Silence prevailed. Sirens and alerts never sounded. With its one hundred and sixty rooms, with its own theatre and chapel, where the parish priest celebrated the mass, with its enormous, one hundred forty-two acre park that stretched into the forests of the Vértes mountain range, and with its immeasurable art treasures and wealth, the manor house knew nothing about the war. (Not so later on.)

In any case, everyone there was getting ready for the arrival of the English. Until that occurred, they were under the protection of the Swiss. On the roof of the manor house was a red cross on a canvas twenty meters long, so that if planes should dive at the village, they could see that they were not allowed to target it. Countess Méri, the grand dame's spinster daughter, was an organizer of Red Cross Hospitals. Just as in the previous war, everyone knitted for the soldiers, sweaters and other things. Just as in the previous World War.

Mama's apartment was located in one of the side-wings of the manor house. It was a spacious room with an enormous, very beautiful tile stove that was heated from the outside, walls three-feet thick, and windows with green shutters; our room opened from it. It was a slightly longish room, János's room when he was a student, stiffly and austerely furnished. In Mami's room, the two conjugal beds still stood beside each other as in times long past. They were covered with a huge cream-colored flag made of wool fabric. In its center was the

Austrian-Hungarian coat-of-arms, which was enclosed by these words: *Indivisibiliter ac inseparabilite.*[17]

The large, marble-slabbed lavatory contained two recessed, small, hand-painted washbasins beside each other. It had an oval tub for washing the feet, also made of hand-painted porcelain. Shepherd boys and girls danced on its rim.

The manor house had no bathrooms. (Maybe one, for Countess Méri.) Every morning, they delivered cold water in one can, hot in another. The toilets were the English type; a boy employed for this purpose filled their tanks with water from a water pot every morning. I remember, we had to tell him there were now three of us, and the water tank would have to be filled more frequently.

Breakfast, tea, lunch, and dinner were brought to us, but nobody ever came in with them. They put them down outside in the entrance and knocked softly. We knew from the time of day that boiling water, lunch, or dinner had arrived. By the time I went out, nobody was in sight. Either this was the practice at the manor house, or Mami had conditioned them to do so.

We set out the unwashed dishes on a tray; they were taken away and brought back without our ever knowing anyone had been there. In the little entrance we found the mail, laundered clothing, and messages on slips of paper. It was Mami's responsibility to take care of the wild raspberries, mulberries, and strawberries wrapped in green leaves in little baskets for the ladies' table. Occasionally, the Esterházys or the chef sent me gifts and daintier morsels.

When I went for a walk, someone tidied up our place, or was it Mami and she just kept it from me? The tower clock was located directly above us. It struck the quarter hours in beautiful, sonorous tones; a little peal of bells preceded them. The clock and pealing bells sounded every fifteen minutes night and day.

I had nothing to do. (The large library contained no Hungarian literature, absolutely none.) János was taciturn, Mami hard of hearing. It was very quiet, only the clock struck continuously. János did not come near me in bed.

My, those evening meals the three of us consumed! Now and then, Mami glances at me, smiling; János reads the newspaper, and we turn in. Mami comes in and kisses me; she stands at the foot of my bed and looks at me, smiling, "You know what I've been thinking? I'll get you a little kitty, I see you are bored here." Then she leaves. She greets János; he mutters something in return. He continues to read, I wait endlessly. Then he turns off the light, does not say good night, and does not even look to see what I am doing. Whenever I try to say something, he interrupts. "What is your problem? People are dying and you want to be huffy about something. Aren't you ashamed?"

By that time I suspected I had caught the infection from him. Had I hurt his feelings, had he become disgusted with me? If he did not love me, why did he marry me? I did not want to get married; I always longed to go to the university and become a doctor. He had persuaded me to marry him with great difficulty. We were already engaged when I suggested to him several times that we not marry, that I become his mistress and attend the university. (I am still very proud of this; this is no big thing today, but back then, fifty years ago, it required great courage and inner freedom.)

I brooded endlessly over János's behavior; I don't know how to express in writing how greatly I suffered.

One time we went up to Budapest, and I met with my mother and my sister and brother, Irénke and Egon, who fled first to Kecskemét and then from there to Budapest. They did not know anything about our father, either. He went off somewhere; they did not find him and thought he was staying with us. (What did he do? He grew drowsy; he was bored with all the commotion, went to his former office girl's place, and lay down to sleep. Then, shucks, well, he just stayed there conveniently, and selling the furnishings from two apartments and two offices, from which he also supported his former mistress, he lived a comfortable life. Oh yes, he did worry about us in the meantime, but he put his faith in God. But more about all these matters in due course.) It felt wonderful to be with my mother, sister, and brother. I also met with Pál Kovács.

How happy we were when an air alert caught us on Museum Boulevard! Well, let's go into the first cellar and have a good heart-to-heart talk! We did that, and we laughed a lot between distant explosions.

Another time, I was walking with Pál and Irénke; we became very hungry. We went into a restaurant. They only had lecsó, nothing else. It burned so much we nearly went crazy; we pleaded in vain, each of us could have only one slice of bread. Drink a lot of water, the waiter advised us, putting a pitcher of water on the table. We laughed with the waiter and drank the water.

I wanted to tell my mother I wished to remain with them, but I could not say anything, and I was still anxious about János's safety. (He was by then considered to be a deserter.) Everyone envied us for having such a safe and good place.

We were going back to Csákvár. We said good-bye to my mother. The poor dear's heart was very heavy. She did not know what had become of father, Egon was a deserter, and Irénke was afraid of the Russians and wanted to go to the West on a hospital train. (She did leave the following day.) My mother hugged me, "I am so happy I don't have to worry about you," she said. She was grateful to János and pleased he had transported her precious darling to such a good place.

These were the quiet, drowsy weeks in the very middle of the war: only the clock struck. I could barely hang on. I went on foot to the Fehérvár highway and stared and stared at the military vehicles passing by; now I will wave and climb aboard, I will leave. Nothing was more simple than that; everyone was fleeing to the West, and everybody found a place there. But I didn't want to go to the West, and it wasn't possible to return to Transylvania. I did know one thing: it was possible to give anything a try, but going back across the front was out of the question. If that was the case, then so be it, but I had to escape from here, no matter where. I boarded one of the vehicles, then got off after a few kilometers, and walked back, dragging my feet. I didn't have a single article of underwear with me, and I wasn't able to buy any clean linen for myself.

I had to go to Székesfehérvár for an examination to see if the infection was gone. The dermatology and venereal disease section of the hospital was located quite some distance from the city. When I gave the particulars about myself, the doctor said, "So you come from Kolozsvár!" With that he ran and fetched Elli Kristóf (the daughter of a local professor), who had left Kolozsvár earlier. For heaven's sake, give me news about Kolozsvár, is her family alive? I felt very ashamed of myself. I mumbled something about "GO" (this was the discrete abbreviation for the disease), but Elli paid no attention, she just kept hugging me and asking questions.

I wanted to leave, but they would not let me – the hospital car would take me to the city. Anyway, the air alert would coincide with the departure time of the passenger bus. That was the rule; in case of an alert, the bus left a half hour after the alert ended. Only, the bus, knowing the time for the alert was approaching, left ahead of schedule, and for this reason, I would not be able to return to Csákvár. I did not consider that such a great tragedy: János and Mami would learn that the bus had departed earlier; they would realize I had missed it.

I did not want to go back to the hospital, it was just too far away. I looked for a hotel. Nothing was available. I came across a young female teacher who was fleeing. We wandered about together. We laughed a lot. If the slightest opportunity presented itself to do so, I was immediately mirthful. (János could not stand it.) We had dinner somewhere, but we did not have a place to stay. Nothing was available, not in the entire town. We wanted to sleep in an easy chair in the lobby of one of the hotels, but the concierge would not let us.

Outside, the cold, the mud, and the alert awaited us. Then a Hungarian army officer gave us his room. He slept in the easy chair, the two of us went up to the room. I felt the sink was so filthy, I didn't even wash up; I lay down without removing my clothes, not wanting the slightly soiled bed linen to touch my skin. The young woman, however, washed and cleaned herself up happily, now that she had, at long last, some running water available and was sleeping in a real bed.

See, I thought, every time I set out to leave Csákvár for good, fear held me back. How will I buy clean clothing? Where are the washrooms located? It wasn't hunger I feared; it was dirt. What a laugh.

We reckoned with the possibility that the officer who gave us his room would perhaps demand something in exchange. Laughing, we barricaded the door. But we never saw the young Hungarian again. We had only exchanged a few words in the lobby. When had he last slept in a real bed? And how many more times would he during his lifetime?

The next day, just as we were having our breakfast, when I looked out, I saw János, unshaven, pale, and haggard, standing before the window that extended to the floor, looking at me. I choked.

Our laughter froze. The three of us engaged in polite conversation for a while. Then we said good-bye.

On the way, János said, "I thought you had run away. I went to your wardrobe right away. Your clothes were there. That meant nothing, of course. I counted your underwear, not one was missing (well, at least he knows how many undergarments I have). Then I thought something had come up, and you were unable to make it back. Mami cried all night, we stirred up the whole town on the telephone, nobody knew a thing about you."

"And what about you?" I asked pointedly, the world slowly turning around with me. "You could break your habit of asking stupid questions," he said. I was amazed he knew I was unhappy. And he knew I would not leave without a change of underwear. I did not speak about this, or about anything, ever, to anyone. In those days, I still kept everything to myself.

We went hunting in Csákvár occasionally. I enjoyed hunting immensely. I played Vicki dog. Clapping, jumping, clattering, I galloped along the base of thickets and precipices driving out the game. It was wonderful. János usually shot down some of the game I routed out. At the sound of the shot, I always stopped for an instant and shouted to him, "Did you hit it?" "A rabbit," he replied precisely, objectively.

He was an excellent shot. I don't think he ever sensed I hoped that maybe now, *now* he had missed. But he almost always hit the target. We ate plenty of pheasant breast. If it was cold, I liked it, too.

He looked down on me a bit for not being able to shoot game. He forced me to for a time; then he noticed that I would aim very carefully, but when I pulled the trigger, I would shut my eyes from fright, only to open them hoping that maybe I had missed. He was much amused and laughed more heartily than he ever had at any other time. Then he let the matter rest. He allowed I was a docile, faithful, and obedient hunting dog.

58

I drove the game with pounding heart. I was so happy, it was such great fun; but one part of me watched uneasily.

One time, I found a pheasant hen at the base of a thicket, poised very close. I clapped and shouted in vain; it would not budge. I ran at it. It moved away a bit, but did not fly up. I shouted to János, maybe it was sick and unable to fly. He laughed jeeringly, saying I was not enough like a dog.

I scared it once more, it was poised very close. The thought that maybe it didn't want to die flashed through me, and in the lovely silence, I bent down and extended my hand toward her, "If you want to live, little bird, I shall let you." At that moment she flew up. János shot her.

We once went hunting with young Mátyás Esterházy, who was home on furlough for a few days. We came across him and went on together for hours. I did not drive the game; János never let me do so in the presence of strangers. I just pushed along with them the entire afternoon. We did not have a dog with us, however. They dropped in on a farmer. The going had become difficult for me because of the large mud boots clinging to our feet. I was already worn out, anyway. János told me to go back and wait for them at the mill; they would be doubling back in a minute.

The Gurd mill was a long-abandoned mill with a water-wheel on the shore of a small, romantic lake and a large waterfall right next to it. The Esterházys had converted it into a summer place; now it was all locked up. I stood on the bridge, listening to the thundering waterfall. I grew tired of waiting for them. I turned around and saw them moving away on the road, leaving the mill. For a moment, it seemed unthinkable. Are they leaving me here? Can it be they have forgotten about me? But they must have seen me standing on the bridge when they approached the mill. The road they came and moved away on passed by at a distance of twenty meters from where I was standing

At first I wanted to stay put; then the foggy autumn forest frightened me – there were no leaves, just bare trees; night was falling, and it was cold, I did not know the way home. I ran after them.

Count Matyi said they had shouted but I had not heard them, certainly because of the noisy waterfall, and "János did not want us to go to you." (What was it he didn't want to do? And why not? Did he balk at the twenty meters? Or at expressing concern for me? What did he think I would do? Look for them? Or try to go home through the unfamiliar, darkening forest? I did not say anything to him; he would not reply, anyway.)

On one of those interminable Sunday afternoons, Mami took me into the "Chamber of Treasures," to experience some kind of pleasure, to entertain me. We stepped into the narrow room on the ground floor facing our part of the manor house. Here candelabra stood in rows, gold and silver candelabra. In the next room were gold and silver plates decorated with engravings or embossings, sets for travel, services for weddings, practical objects, jewel chests, mirrors, statues, and ciboria. We continued on and on until we reached the jewelry. This represented not just wealth, but beauty and art.

I was about to drown when I happened upon a lifesaver. They turned the convent's hospital for the poor into a military emergency hospital. Against every objection from János I arranged with Sister Franciska to report for work there every day.

In the three higher forms of high school, I had worked as a nurse during summer and winter vacations. I had completed three months of training in surgery, and was myself serving as a nursing instructor. (When I had to undo a freshly amputated leg from its dressings for the first time, to hold it while the surgeon was cutting around the shredded flesh without having administered an anesthetic, and afterwards to bind it up again, my clothing became saturated with sweat, but I quickly got used to it.)

In any case, I knew much more than the local personnel and the nuns, and had greater practical experience. But they handled me very gingerly, like someone from the manor house who was simply "bored."

I took temperatures, prepared sponges, and wrote reports on the patients. When Sister Franciska found out that I occasionally performed physical labor – for instance, that I tidied up the place – she strongly objected and ordered the others not to let me do it.

The patients called me little nurse, the others madam. In short, I was a carefully handled "ornament". In that village, just living in the shadow of the manor house was considered a very great thing.

Of course, appearances also indicated this: I arrived at the hospital in my arctic-fox fur coat, fur cap, and top boots, like an elegant lady. But I took them off, and my clothes too, and slipped into a white smock and flat cap. Nuns and male doctors worked at the hospital exclusively; the cook was the only civilian woman besides myself.

The patients were all very nice. One of them asked me to chat with him because I resembled his wife. Another to speak to him in Rumanian.

One time, the chief physician gave a patient from a forced labor camp, a young, swarthy man, a good tongue-lashing. He did not utter a single word in response, nor did any of the others. (It was a military hospital, but still...) When the doctor left the ward, a profound silence arose. I went over to the youth's bed and sat down beside him for a few minutes. We talked about trivial things, but I felt that everyone considered it good; they knew why I did it.

The weeks passed. The hospital was without bread. Much running, hurrying around went on. I told Countess Méri about it, and she had foodstuff sent to the hospital for a week. A hundred kilos of bread, fifty kilos of butter, four wagon loads of potatoes – this did not mean trouble for the manor house. They felt very grateful at the hospital, and they treated me even more gingerly.

The front drew nearer. Casualties arrived in mounting numbers. We ran out of pharmaceuticals; we used paper for bandages; the wounded lay on straw mattresses on the floor, then on straw only, often alongside each other. Confusion was at its peak. The doctors tended the wounded only, to the point of complete exhaustion.

They left internal medicine to me, all of it. We had no medicine, no x-ray, no space, no food, but we still had to do something. Desperately ill, unconscious patients were delivered incessantly. What a struggle it was! I was by then also working in the operating room; I became the chief surgeon's right hand.

I prepared two reports on each of the dead twice, and discharged in the place of each of them a living person who was ambulatory and had somewhere to flee to. Of course, someone like that needed civilian clothes and false documents. Shoes were the greatest worry. I had to account for the boots of the dead – where would I get hold of so many boots? – and fugitives had to wear something on their feet.

Then a brilliant idea struck us, I mean the patients and me. I reported that during the night an unidentified thief had stolen the boots of all the patients in internal medicine. (We had stolen and hidden them as a reserve supply.) My, what a commotion erupted! For, while the doctors and nurses were perishing from work, administrative employees found plenty of time for everything. They investigated and investigated.

I don't think I was aware of the risk I was taking. After all, this was the military; such an act meant execution by firing squad. This never occurred to me.

I did not speak to János about the matter.

The soldiers apparently knew about it, but they kept silent to protect me. Even now my eyes fill with tears when I think of them. These sad, defenseless, sick bodies – what a gallows humor they had; how able they were to die silently, wordlessly; how grateful they were for the slightest bit of attention.

Not one of them ever offended me with a single gesture, a word. I was the only woman among one hundred, then a hundred and fifty men, and they always treated me with affection and respect. If a new patient arrived and swore or used any rude words in my presence, the others instantly rebuked him. However, I never wanted them to restrain themselves because of me; they were suffering enough.

I could relate many more things about this hospital and its patients. You can revile the Hungarians as much as you please, I will never believe you. These unfortunate soldiers could be so magnificent amid all that wretchedness, with death close by, abiding inside them, and threatening them from the outside. Meanwhile, the Russians were drawing closer; the Germans or Szálasi's men[18] were slaughtering whoever deserted (a bullet in the head immediately); they knew nothing about their families, their homes, not even what they were fighting for. I experienced one of the most dreadful days of my life at this hospital.

Four little boys playing on the street found a hand grenade. They threw it against the side of a house and waited to see what would happen. One died instantly, the other three were brought in to us. We took them to the dressing station. The intestines of one of them hung out of his open abdominal wall; his teeth and cheekbone showed nakedly, both his eyes draining out. We laid two of them on the dressing table, one on the examining couch. Dr. Horváth, the internal specialist, administered first aid; I assisted him. Our surgeons were in Fehérvár. What could be done? Injections of pain-killers and coagulants, sponging.

I dashed to the telephone and asked for Fehérvár on a special line to have a surgeon come immediately. I could not locate ours anywhere; I pleaded for any military or private surgeon whatsoever. Interestingly, no one said you must be insane, you must be out of your mind. There is a war going on. (Would I have dared to call the military doctors back from Fehérvár or anywhere else for adults?)

I assisted with the preparations for surgery and returned to the dressing station. We waited with the three children from nine in the morning until four in the afternoon.

The frantic parents arrived about ten o'clock. They waited for two hours. Then they wanted to see their children. They were mistrustful, they wanted to know what was going on. They wanted to see them even if they were dying.

How could we permit a mother to go to her mangled child when all we were doing was waiting and nothing was happening? (And when the children recognized their parents' voices, if they recognized them, what did that gesture mean?) The mother of the child whose intestines hung out, an inn-keeper's wife, with a large behind and hips and big bosom, a known prostitute, began to pound on the door frantically about twelve o'clock; she wanted to break in and see her son.

"Let's give the child a large dose of morphine," I begged Horváth. "I cannot, medical ethics prohibits it." "Then I will do it," I said, preparing the dose, but he did not let me. They cannot save him anyway, I whispered – because I was afraid the child would understand me – and if they did, what kind of life would he have? Poor Horváth. He did not argue, he did not explain. "No." He motioned for me to leave if I could not bear it any longer.

We did not know what to do with the parents. We wrestled them to the floor and stopped up their mouths – the inn-keeper's wife[19] bellowed – we dragged her into the woodshed and anesthetized her. I returned to the children. (Dear God, are you looking down upon this?)

Actually, was it my nerves that could not bear it, or did I want death for the sake of the children and their parents? And if I had the chance, would I have administered the morphine? Would I have killed the child?

I don't exactly know where I stand regarding death. The following happened two years ago. A young Gypsy was dying, and I felt very sorry for him. When I went on duty in the isolation ward in the morning, the night nurse said, "He died at four o'clock, don't go in." I went in, anyway, full of fear. I wanted to get used to it. I stood in the room for a moment and then looked at him. A feeling of soft serenity and pure tranquility came over me, even though he was a grinning, ugly corpse.

It is possible that my nerves could not bear it.

Before long, the hospital had to move on because Csákvár was being evacuated for some strategic reason. It turned out that I was considered to be a member of the hospital's staff and had to go with them.

Dr. Horváth asked me whether I was going or staying. I knew it was all over; I knew we had to lose the war, and we were anxiously waiting for the Russians or the English. I saw no point in escaping. On the other hand, I would have liked to get away from the manor house, chiefly from János. And I felt I could be helpful if I went with the staff. I liked to work. In short, I did not know what to do.

Dr. Horváth told me softly, as always, that if I did not go with them, that would mean execution by a firing squad, that court martial was in force. Execution by a firing squad was the consequence of so many things that you did not even pay any attention to it. He added, just as softly, "I would like you to come with us, but I think you should stay, it will be better for you that way."

I stayed.

A long time before this crisis, I went to Székesfehérvár one late afternoon. By that time it was clear to us that the front was coming dangerously close. It could have been some kind of Catholic holiday (at the time I was still a Protestant); the church was crammed with flowers and packed with people; they were burning incense and singing in the warmth, over and over again, irresistibly:

> *Blessed Mother, our great ancient Patroness!*
> *Alone in deep distress, our country hails thee thus:*
> *Do not forget Hungary, our dear homeland,*
> *Do not forget the poor Hungarians!*

They wept and sang, candles were burning; they pleaded with Mary to protect Hungary or, at least, Székesfehérvár. Could anyone resist such supplication, I thought, filled with anguish, and I began to feel frightened. I was still unacquainted with the horrors that were to come.

Later, when Székesfehérvár changed hands several times, the Russians, after first raping them, cut off with knives the breasts of the women who had cohabited with the Germans.

I had no idea of such horrors; still, there in the church, I felt an ominous fate hanging above the region, the place. This was the first moment that a dreadful terror seized me. I wept and prayed. Then I left the church, and I thought that the spell was caused by mass hypnosis, that I had become impressionable. We were expecting all this ultimately; somehow, we will make it through the period of the front and the war will be over.

But still, I grew ever more afraid.

Mami was deaf. She ran the household with complete meticulousness. János did not speak; above us, the clock chimed every quarter of an hour. The hospital moved out. The manor house lived a life of seemingly immutable orderliness and cleanliness.

All bottlenecks and difficulties halted at the entrance of the manor house park. I played with the kitten and listened to the fear reverberating inside me. I was completely alone, as a wife of six months, loving and feeling out of place beside my own husband.

I did not know anyone in the village. I did not even see anyone who lived in the manor house.

Captives were being taken through the village. Not taken but herded. I gave my angora scarf to one of them. Mami shook her head, János reprimanded me for giving away that one instead of an old one. "Does it make any difference?" I replied. "We will never have any scarves again." János said I was crazy.

By now, I had to confine myself to home. Occasionally, I took a walk in the park. János no longer slept with me; he did not even speak to me. Mami was quiet, sweet. Once in a while, János grumbled that the food was awful. Only later did we find out how good it was. At the time, I already had a highly favorable opinion of it, though it was quite different from Transylvanian cooking. On the other hand, back home we had long lived on bread, sugar, and meat ration cards. We drank linden-blossom tea with saccharine, made a sandwich spread out of yeast and flour, and kept rabbits so there would be some meat. My mother struggled, but the moment we sat down at the dining room table, we cheerfully ate whatever was before us.

Many guests showed up at the Esterházys. The cook was angry – too many guests, too much work for her. They sent us delicacies, both the mistress of the house and the chef. The chef cooked for the lord of the manor and his family, and a woman cooked for the indoor staff of thirty servants. The coachmen, gardeners, grooms, janitors, stableboys, the chauffeur, and various experts formed the outdoor staff; they did not live in the house. I don't know where they took their meals. But I do know that every blessed day was prepared a very rich soup with meat, noodles or dumplings in a kettle, followed by pasta or leavened dough, so that in case some woman in the village fell ill, she and her family could have lunch, as well as every person in need who just happened to be passing through.

The employees of the Esterházy family all bought houses and land for their old age (Mami did this, too), vineyards at an early age, with wine cellars. They could raise their children securely.

The Esterházys had an ample supply of employees, a forestry office for their woods, a game preserve, a dairy farm with six hundred cows, and so on. The estate consisted of just over eight thousand five hundred acres, the entailed property of thirty-four thousand and eighty acres.

The manorial cooking was, in my opinion, the very worst.

Every soup was put through a sieve, and after that, it was strained through loosely woven, snow-white (diaper-like) cloths. It was barely seasoned, you could not even tell what you were eating. The meats were wonderfully decorated, like an embroidered tablecloth, but saltless, flat to the taste. The pies, the layer cakes, the pastries were so sweet I could not swallow them.

It was a great privilege and very thoughtful on their part to share their food with us, but I could not enjoy it, even ate it reluctantly. What shall I do? Mami just stared at me, smiled, shook her head, removed my plate, and hid it somewhere.

The chef had his own female cook at his home. He had food prepared separately for himself; he partook of that (I am not surprised). He, too, sent us snacks from time to time.

The cooking for the staff was the best. Something always turned up. Sometimes they butchered a pig for the staff, and pig-killing lunches and suppers were served; sometimes we also butchered one for ourselves with Mami. (Only to have some to send to the family.) The forestry office sent us wild boar marinated, smoked, raw, frozen under rocks; its color was ruby red. It had to be eaten sliced paper-thin.

If we went hunting, we would bring home so many rabbits and partridges that we could barely cope with cooking them. Mami larded the quail and pheasant breasts with bacon and then roasted them. Now and then, we longed for plainer fare, so we baked potatoes sprinkled with butter and caraway to crispness in the oven for ourselves. We cooked only for our own diversion.

Nyunyuka, our Siamese cat whose original name was Zaime, was still living with us. She ate only pure, raw beef, and she could not stand dogs. She immediately attacked whenever she spotted a dog. Nyunyuka was a domesticated wild animal; Countess Méri had received her as a gift. They entrusted her to Mami's care, then no one ever so much as took a look at her again.

I remember, I once came across a curious-looking purse-like object at Mami's. I opened it; it contained small, white, round plates. I took hold of one of them and asked Mami what it was. To which Mami said, laughing a little, "Oh, you must not touch it, you will defile it. It is the wafer that is given during Holy Communion; hands must not touch it." With that, she put it back and closed the box.

I got together with Monika Esterházy once in a while; we fooled around quite merrily. It was still possible to laugh with her when I went to Majk or she came over. Mami's relative, Uncle Feri, was the chef at the manor house in Majk. But the gap between Monika's way of life and mine was insurmountable. Not because Monika was a countess; it did not matter that I was a relative of the local housekeeper and their chef. A lively, democratic life was in full swing at the manor house in Majk. The count's four offspring, Mátyás, Menyus, Marcell and Monika, grew up, played, and fought with the children of the staff. I came to know Monika in my childhood, and I once spent a few days at Majk while János was at the front. She pummeled, tickled, and hugged me.

At Majk, the servants and part of the indoor staff lived in the former Camaldul monastery near the Gothic church. Each of these charming little empires was situated in a small courtyard enclosed by stone walls, in a house built of ashlar with a room to the right, one to the left and a narrow corridor in the middle. During my stay as a guest, I slept in the manor house, but I had lunch with my future relative, Uncle Feri, in one such house. It was terribly hot, a midday in August. We were getting ready to sit down to the table when my cousin said, "Móni, get a pitcher of water for the lunch." She replied, "I'll go crazy running to the well in this heat to haul water." To this my cousin said, "Have you no shame at all? My father has been cooking for you since this morning, so a white-gloved valet can wait on you, and you won't even bring us a pitcher of water?" Without a word, Monika took the pitcher and ran for the water. This was the atmosphere at the manor house in Majk.

But what could we talk about together now? I quickly became bored with the fraternization.

Uncle Feri, the former chef at Majk, once looked me up in Budapest at the time of the democracy. After the war, as he was sitting on a train, a piece of debris had hit the window and half of his arm had to be amputated. At the first moment, when I opened the door, I mistook him for a beggar, he was so shabby, with a satchel attached to his shoulder. He told me that when the Russians reached Majk, the mistress of the manor rolled up her sleeves and began cooking for two hundred men! She was an excellent cook. "Well, what do you say to that?" he said, "I am a chef, but I could not cook like that for an army corps. And she always gave them a good bawling-out if they kicked up a row in the manor house. Monika took care of the horses. There was no trouble for a time, because they drained out all the wine in anticipation, emptying it all into the creeks."

Monika – so I heard – became a wagon driver, then wound up in Vienna.

Now, in 1989, she is the friend of a friend of mine, and helps her with true generosity of heart. (I must look her up in Vienna.)

About ten years ago, Miklós and I and some German friends of ours went to Uncle Feri's house – or one like it. Some old lady was living there. Rags on the sofa, poverty and dirt in the house, several dogs and cats with their smell. The old lady, who had seen much better days, looked like a beggar. But she did not complain or express any bitterness; she received us kindly and animatedly. She chatted as if we were seated in the drawing room of the manor house, as if we were at Majk.

One time, before the front arrived, we came upon the young lady in the park; she was driving the horses. She stopped the wagon, showed interest, and kept asking questions. We also asked how she was. "Very well," she replied sincerely, spiritedly. Her husband was a prisoner at Sopronkőhida, one of her sons had disappeared, and she did not know a thing about the others. This is what they were like, and this is what they remained.

THE FRONT

It was already winter, and the front came closer and closer to Csákvár. Time passed at a snail's pace. Then the Germans arrived.

One morning, they burst into the manor house. "Orders! You have to leave!" How? On what? I set out to negotiate with the Germans, taking into account that any of the others would get a bullet in the head. Not Mami. She knew German, but when she heard we had to leave the manor, she started to cry, her entire body shook; she cried and cried and then got diarrhea, as she always did when she was nervous.

I asked them to provide cars for our little band of ten in exchange for a side of pork, so we could go to the forester's lodge with our belongings.

I could not speak German, just a few words, and only a smattering of French. Soldiers wearing top boots conducted me to the command post. To my surprise, they had set up quarters at the manor house. I was able to enter at once, and I somehow made myself understood. The Germans granted my request; they did not ask me who the ten persons were; maybe they knew and just let us take flight. The jeeps arrived quickly at the side entrance of the manor. We packed up our belongings. Belongings? This meant our personal things, warm clothing; then mattresses, rugs, pillows, bedspreads, furs, utensils, food; next the house altar, the ciborium, the host, wines, and so on. The jeeps made many trips to the lodge and back.

The Esterházys rolled out huge barrels of wine and knocked out the bottoms with axes, and the wine ran into the creek. They knew the reason why. People raced to the spot with buckets. The Germans were furious, but they bit their tongues.

We dumped everything onto the floor of the half-empty forester's lodge, which was located at the base of the mountain, at Pusztakőhányás. The commotion was immense; it was raining and mud was everywhere. (It must have been one of the milder days of winter.) Then we hitched horses to the wagons and drove them up the mountain to the upper forester's lodge. We didn't tell the Germans where we were heading; it was better if they did not know, and they did not ask us.

We transported the French prisoners of war and the Jews first because they were in immediate danger. German soldiers lent us a helping hand at the time we boarded the jeeps; I do not think we roused any suspicion. They saw what was going on (for example, the French could not speak Hungarian), but they gave no sign of noticing anything. Then we went on the wagons from Pusztakőhányás up to Mindszentpuszta, into the Vértes mountain range.

Mindszentpuszta consisted of a forester's lodge and some auxiliary buildings: a summer kitchen, a stable, a kennel, and some lumber rooms. The house itself was quite small; a couple of steps led to an open veranda (an outhouse at its end). The kitchen opened from a little vestibule with a room to the right, another to the left. At Countess Esterházy's order, we had taken with us their most valuable hunting dogs, sixteen in number, their favorite saddle horses, many valuable hunting weapons, furs, lots of provisions, and sides of pork. Since – as I have related – the Esterházys quickly opened the wine cellars at the time the Germans arrived, pouring several thousand liters of wine into the courtyard, and people carried away the expensive bottled specialities, we naturally could help ourselves to whatever we wanted. We placed the wines and an assortment of hard liquors in sealed, waxed, moldy bottles into several straw-lined cases. (As a direct consequence, we were tipsy in the evenings at Mindszentpuszta. This made our moods more tolerable – for a while.) We took Nyunyuka with us, too, our Siamese cat. Hating dogs, she attacked a German officer's dog to scratch out its eyes. A dog is completely defenseless at such a time. It tore around whining and howling. The German soldiers watched, dumbfounded; we finally captured the dog and scraped off its head the wildly snarling Nyunyuka, her eyes now a fiery red, then stuffed her into a covered basket with great difficulty.

I don't remember what else we took with us. Nothing of very special value. I did want to take away a codex that was lying on the floor, but I felt embarrassed, thinking I would be stealing it. I put it back on the shelf. I don't know what became of the silver and gold objects and the precious stones. I did not ask Mami or the Esterházys about them during later meetings. Events rushed at us so fast that these matters completely faded from our consciousness.

I did hear later that on the night we left, the Germans got drunk and threw glasses of jam against the frescoes, shattered the Chinese porcelain dishes, and shot up the etched mirrors.

Mami still had to assist with the liquidation of the estate, and stayed behind with the understanding that she would follow us after a few days. I myself didn't want to go to the Vértes mountain range. I preferred to move into Mami's little peasant house in the village, but they rejected this plan. In the forester's lodge we shall, they said, get through it all without being detected.

By the time we reached Pusztakőhányás, all of us looked like real refugees. Everyone was sitting on their own baggage; rain was falling in torrents outside. We released Nyunyuka from the basket: the dogs, locked in one of the rooms, barked and whimpered. We prayed that they would not run into the cat.

I stumbled upon a cylindrical box out in the mud on the ground. I picked it up and opened it; it contained a beautiful piece of goldsmith's work, a ciborium. The Yugoslav priest had lost it. He was happy I found it; we celebrated mass daily. We had with us a lovely Italian corpus made of ivory, in the lower part of a crucifix of Lebanese cedar, a small piece of bone from some saint in a little gold compartment. This comprised the sacrament; later it became the family altar. Some in the group turned very morose because I had touched the communion chalice of the Mass with my blasphemous Protestant hands. I was the only Protestant in the whole company. However surprising it may seem, we were at this time the "secretaries" of the Papal nunciature, since with us was Pál Förstner, the embassy secretary, whom we had to hide because of his Jewish lineage. We had in our possession the papal flag and an enameled plaque inscribed in three languages, "Papal Nunciature, Diplomatic Corps. Extra-territorial, Inviolable." Later this took root in me very clearly, "*Exterritorialis.*" Also written in the Cyrillic alphabet was, "*Diplomatiicheski corpus.*" If the Germans only knew.... We were, the others believed, prepared for any and all eventualities. I believed no such thing. Somewhere inside me, I sensed, I knew that tragic events were approaching. We were not able to avoid anything. The absolutely indifferent and odd manner in which János was treating me and the loss of my family and Transylvania added to my anxiety. I couldn't talk to a single member of the group; after all, I had hardly seen any of them , and certainly had not spoken to any of them. The manor house was like a city; you didn't know those who lived in a distant wing. Transylvania – only later did I sense how much this meant – jealously guarded the old traditions of an ancient religious freedom and its own special brand of democracy. Until then, I hadn't had any inkling of the type of religious tension that now encompassed me. (For example, when I found the chalice, one of the party stepped up to me and coldly took it out of my hand. "Why did you open it?" "I stepped on it in the mud, and I did not know what the oddly shaped box could possibly be," I replied. "Even so, you should not have handled it; this is a sacrament." "Then it shouldn't have been lost," I replied, still innocently and in a really friendly way, and with that, I moved on.)

The others were huddled together; by now only János and I were doing any hauling. We made several round trips and fetched mattresses, bedding, cooking utensils, and who knows what else. Next came the wagons to which we hitched the coach horses. Not used to yokes, they did not want to pull. Cursed at, whipped on the narrow, precipitous road in torrential rain, the horses turned wild; they galloped, kicked with their hind legs, tugged at the wagon fiercely, so it got stuck, leaning to the side.

János unexpectedly put the reins in my hands, jumped off and, yelling, whipped the horses with all his might. They neighed, reared, kicked their hind legs, but they refused to pull. It was hellish. I was so frightened I almost screamed, but I held on to the reins without a word. When the horses started out wildly with a jerk, I almost tumbled between them. Everything rattled and creaked. I did know something about driving horses; but there was absolutely no possibility I would be able to guide these wild monsters on the dark forest road in the torrential downpour. I didn't pray any more; everything in my taut muscles and quivering brain became confused.

When the pace became steadier, János, to rescue us, jumped up onto the driver's seat beside me while we were still moving, and took over the reins. He was very brave and quick. I would have given up the battle long ago and just sat there in the rain, waiting for dawn and something to happen. We reached Mindszentpuszta toward midnight (and we still had several more round trips to make).

Jenő Sneider, the forester, lived in one room with his wife, Katinka and Márton Kerecsendi Kiss and the nineteen-year-old wife of a soldier serving at the front, a forester, in the other. She was called Ilonka. They received us kindly and very affectionately. The others picked their way up to the place on shorter footpaths.

I have one more special memory of this night. The coach horses had to be taken back to Csákvár. We were taking two horses into the stable on a ramp, and I was leading the way with a candle I protected against the wind with a paper funnel. I slipped, dropped the candle, and rolled under the horses' legs in the pitch-dark. Without even slowing down, the two horses stepped over me without doing me the least harm, even though I was, meanwhile, rolling downwards under them. János, on the other hand, stepped on me with his booted foot. Swearing furiously, he picked me up from the ground. "Have you gone mad? How can anyone be so clumsy!" He didn't even take the trouble to comfort me; he didn't even bother to ask whether the horses had kicked me or not. I wonder whether he knew these animals were this sensitive and quick and was not worried for that reason. Or did he think I would have cried out if I had been injured? Apart from annoyance, he showed no sign of any emotion. Possibly I was clumsy, but what city-bred woman would have handled it any better? On the whole, I must confess, I look back today on these accomplishments of mine appreciatively. I have been chicken-hearted, indeed cowardly, longer than I care to remember. Back then I only put on a brave face because I was under too much stress to feel fear. At Mindszentpuszta, they made beds on the floor of the forester's lodge toward dawn. János and I lay together, sharing a mattress. He didn't speak to me. Everyone said good night, but he didn't.

He did not embrace me, did not even touch me. He pulled away and turned his back to me. I thought he must be angry about something. But what? Because I'd been so clumsy with the horses? Because of the "infection"? Did he hate me because I had venereal disease? I could think of no other reason. After all – though I will not dwell on it here – I surrounded him with love, attention, and tenderness. I also tried to figure out what he was thinking. He hadn't talked with me for weeks by then.

We settled into the forester's lodge. The French went off by themselves, to live in a little place next to the summer kitchen. They cooked for us all. One of them was a meat cook as a civilian; another was also a cook, but he understood pastries only. My task was to supervise the kitchen, manage the supplies, and discuss the menus and other matters with them, apparently because I could speak a little French, and could also do a bit of cooking. Needless to say, if I told them we should make bean soup, they'd prepare some kind of unspeakable dish. We called it "bauxite" soup. (When the dried beans became half soft, they ground them up and then ground some celeriac into it.) They poured scrambled eggs on layered potatoes[20] and so on. Occasionally, they asked permission to fix a real "French" meal. I consented, of course. I remember one of those meals even now. They cooked carrots in salty water, and also some peeled raw potatoes, but first they trimmed them, so that they would have a pretty, uniform oval shape. They arranged them on large round platters, the way we cut cake into slices. A slice of carrot, a slice of white potato. A nicely fried egg on the carrot, a slice of quickly broiled deer liver on top of the potato, round and round the platters. It was beautiful and delicious – in 1944, in the last days of the war!

The bread-baking episode was our record collective achievement. Evoking memories from my childhood, we prepared the leaven in the evening, and kneaded and raised the dough in the morning. When I went with them to put the bread in, the oven was ice cold. (I don't know how they thought we were going to bake it.) The result: a series of little slabs about a meter in diameter.

All this was interesting, and it would have been convenient as well, if they had not been so terribly wasteful. Poor Katinka, Jenő Sneider's wife, felt disheartened. Uncle Jenő, the chief forester, comforted her with great gentleness and wisdom, saying that it is not possible to cook separately for so many people. Who would do the cooking? For whom, where, and on what basis would it be done?

They were an interesting couple. Uncle Jenő was tall, thin, slow-speaking, slow-moving. He was wise, cheerful, serious-minded. Katinka was short, buxom, down to earth, all heart and action. The great love of his life had been Katinka's sister, who played the violin beautifully. She died after a couple of weeks of wedded bliss. After a few years, he married Katinka, who was her exact opposite. After the war, I visited the Sneiders and noticed they had put in a bathtub as tiny as a child's. Uncle Jenő told me that he had searched a long time for one like it, because he heard it was possible to drown in a bathtub, and Katinka always liked taking a bath "that way." We lived through quite dangerous days together, and nothing happened to her. She died three years later while undergoing surgery for appendicitis.

Uncle Jenő was – who knows why – a right-winger; the reason they came to the forester's lodge was to increase their distance from the Russians.

Márton Kerecsendi Kiss arrived with the Sneiders. He had just become a recognized author. He had been János's schoolmate, and it was János who put them in touch with each other. The Sneiders grew very fond of Márton.

When every girl in Transylvania was corresponding with a boy in the home country, I wrote to Marci. Exchanges of photos, and so on. He began to sound the notes of love, at which I quickly informed him I was secretly János's fiancée, thus staving off complications. This past colored our relationship.

Katinka and I immediately became friends as housewives. I have no idea of what they thought about the relationship between János and me, for I never gave the slightest hint to anyone about it. They were all every tactful and observant. They didn't tease us about our being newlyweds, and they didn't try to hush János's cold, grudging voice. Afterwards, I was very grateful to them for this.

What was odd about this friendly company was that a continual political tension existed between us. They believed in a German victory and waited every minute for the front to reverse. We waited every minute for it to come to an end; after all, our very lives depended on it. Only one solution presented itself: no one ever talked politics, we never argued about anything. We talked about literature, philosophy, people, the past. We told stories, we played games. The endless winter nights passed. We opened the expensive bottles one after the other. Some were so old, a fine sediment had settled on the bottom, like moldy tree leaves.

Marci and his wife were anti-Semitic, I believe. They were not pleased in principle by our harboring Jews, but they accepted it in practice. Only one of their requests betrayed their views: they wanted to share a room with us, without any strangers, if possible. So, the others lived in the other room.

Our Siamese cat also lived with us. The dogs? Well, they were the cause of great concern. Only someone who has worked and lived with them could possibly know what taking care of sixteen hunting dogs involved. Förstner, a functionary of the nunciature's secretary, took care of them. We honored him with the title "Le chef de chien." He spoke to them politely, informally, or he swore at them, also very politely. We almost died from laughing. He had never owned a dog in his life. (He was likable, and I was fond of him. He was a short, plump man, always smiling, and he had brown eyes – the exact opposite of his tall, skinny, stern mother. Mina was a short young girl about twenty; she was also short and stocky with heavy bronze-colored hair and with a short, freckled, hysterical mother, whom I didn't like. Mina didn't like the poor thing, either. How on earth could she be like that?)

One time, Nyunyuka went into the Yugoslav priest's Mass, which he celebrated every day. Not wanting to interrupt the liturgy, they did not chase her out, and she settled down at the base of the crucifix. This became her favorite spot. The old priest captured my heart by looking at her, smiling, and saying she could sleep there in peace, except during the Mass. (The crucifix was the monstrance – it was set on top of a writing table.)

In the evenings, the men would go outdoors for a cigarette; Katinka and I would spread the mattresses on the floor and distribute the covers, undress and lie down. Then the men would come in, turn off the light, undress in the dark and lie down. Getting up in the morning followed a similar pattern. The Förstners did the same.

In the middle of the night, a hand grenade exploded in the yard; a round of machine gun fire immediately followed. We jumped out of bed instantly. We ran back and forth. Uncle Jenő and János ordered us women into a corner. (As I found out in the morning, they did that because it was the place best protected from the bullets flying through the window.) They looked outside intently. They wanted to shoot back! They wanted to go out!

Katinka and I implored them not to move and threatened to run after them immediately if they dared to go out. This infuriated them, but eventually they stayed inside.

The men outside were Russian partisans. They had fired only to avoid close combat. They did not want anything of us – they carried away some provisions. A live calf, a side of pork, and the like. The Frenchmen were frightened out of their wits, but they kept quiet. Next to them was a very small room, designated as the supply depot; the partisans drove the calf from the stable. As a result, our stock of provisions decreased sharply.

In the daytime, the men would go hunting. Sometimes I would go with them. It was then that I became acquainted with Filike, a sandy-colored miniature dachshund, one of the Esterházys' most wonderful dogs. He was a descendent of the English royal family. I think this must be taken to mean the canine royal family; no one remains whom I could ask what the case really was. The excitement of the hunters did not affect me, but I was beside myself with pleasure when we walked in the woods, János in front, the dog behind him, I in back. Suddenly, János stopped to listen, and Filike froze with one leg poised in the air. The snow crackled under me. János turned around nervously. "Do pay attention to how a real hunting dog behaves!" I never could please him. I so loved the snowy woods and the dog that I was full of joy; it was for this reason I couldn't always listen attentively and tread cautiously enough. You have to walk in a way that won't scare the game away. You have to step noiselessly when the other person is also taking a step, then stop when the other person stops. It was a strange way to walk, I must say. It seemed to parody my entire marriage. Then, to the great consternation of the others, I began walking in the woods alone instead. What would happen to me if I encountered Russian partisans or straggling soldiers? Or ran into the Russians or the Germans? I tried losing my way many times. I walked in the woods aimlessly, but at sunset fear forced me return to the lodge, humiliated.

(How strange and wonderful life is: a few decades later, I would be riding a *"deux chevaux"* with my husband, Miklós, beside me, through what to me had been such a painful and danger-fraught area, and sipping black coffee in a spuriously ultra-modern espresso in Csákvár.)

János and some of the men once shot a stag. We were again assured of about two hundred pounds of meat. We were delighted. They skinned it and hoisted it high with a pulley, to the top of a post, so it would freeze and animals could not reach it. (This was the customary practice.) We threw a big supper. The next day, the meat, enough for several weeks, was nowhere to be seen. Partisans had taken it, without firing a shot. By then, we were living in close proximity to each other, in what you might call peaceful accord.

One day toward noon, a light buggy stopped in front of the house; in it was a tired woman, Klári, who appeared to be about forty, and her daughter, Marianne, about fourteen – Förstner's relatives. How had they found their way to us and where had they come from? They became our new housemates.

Ilonka, the forester's young wife, was going down to her native village to her mother. I wanted to go with her, no matter what. They let me join her very reluctantly. In addition to a wagon, they provided us with an armed forester for protection.[21] We tipped over within a half an hour; the forester, falling out of the wagon, leaned on the gun barrel. The barrel filled up with sand. Then it could not be fired, because it would explode in our hands. We had a good laugh about this. I had quite an unfortunate fall; half my leg wound up under the wagon, but happily, there was thick, soft snow beneath me; otherwise, my leg would have been broken. I limped slightly but was cheerful and relieved. At such a young age, you are like a little animal; if it is able, it moves and is happy. (All the same, I am like this now, I like being happy.)

We went to a Swabian village. Ilonka's mother told her happily that her husband would be home Saturday on a two-day leave. "He should not go back to the army," I said. "Dress him in civilian clothes and have him wait, hidden somewhere, for the Russians." They looked at me very strangely. They belonged to the Volksbund. A little, pale, whining girl was also in the house; she was about fifteen or sixteen years old, kind of city-like. As it turned out, this Hungarian girl had skipped away from home and was living with a German soldier, and went with him everywhere at the front. Now they were billeted here. She just looked at us; she never spoke a word. (They could easily have broken my neck.)

We were given a substantial lunch, then we had to shoe our horse. Also, we had to get some kerosene and salt. We were barely able to light our lamps. We started out a bit late, and we had also had a little to drink. Night descended upon us quickly; we took another swig to keep from getting cold. We gave no thought either to partisans or to straying lines of soldiers, the front, or other matters; we sang as if we were going to raise the woods. (Of course, at the time I sang just as off-key as always.)

Suddenly, our horse stopped and refused to go on. An exhausted, collapsed horse was lying crosswise at the bottom of the steep road. We could not get it to stand on its legs, and we did not have the strength to run our horse across it. No matter how hard it was beaten, it would not step over the horse, because it knew that then it would pull the wagon across it. We tugged and tugged, but we could not make it step around the spent horse on the narrow, steep road. The thought of the wagon going across the live horse was appalling. Ilonka and I covered our eyes; we stood at a distance, huddled together. We were glad the horse resisted. It did not kick or neigh when being beaten. When pulled by its halter, it reared up. Finally, we unharnessed it; then it quietly stepped over its mate lying on the ground; and we, with great pain and difficulty, half pulled, half lifted the wagon over the sick animal. This scene affected me deeply; later, I wanted to go back for a blanket and some feed, so it would not freeze to death, but I was, of course, not allowed to do so. (It was said that the following day someone picked it up and stood it on its legs; it had collapsed from fatigue. Then the Russians took it away; it could not take that, and died shortly afterwards.)

Half an hour later, we were singing again. Much later, we met some men with lamps; we were immeasurably amazed, because those who frequented the woods lay low, hid behind trees, and crept along on their stomachs. János and the men had come to meet us. They gave way to despair at our having fallen into the hands of partisans. When they heard us droning away, they were driven out of their minds by worry as to who was doing the singing. I jumped out of the wagon and, limping slightly, ran toward them. János grabbed me by the arm and wanted to beat me up – according to Uncle Jenő, only from nervous tension because he was very worried about me. In a strange way, I took this lightly; indeed, it pleased me and I laughed at it. As for the notion that it was stupid and dangerous to be singing, I replied that the contrary was true. It was the rattling wagon that betrayed our passing through the woods, but it was possible to tell from the singing that two tipsy women were driving it, and so it was not worth shooting. Uncle Jenő said I was right, but they strongly curtailed my freedom. I no longer left the lodge alone.

One day, gendarmes came into the forest. They warmed themselves at our place – there was not another lodge within miles. They were combing the woods, exterminating partisans. (I won't record the horrible details.) We gave them a bunch of Russian hand grenades and two Russian machine guns, to enable them to defend themselves in case any new partisans showed up.

Marci called me aside to tell me that a serious problem had developed. Ilonka had let out that János was a deserter, and the gendarmes wanted to take him away. (By then the Szálasi type of massacre[22] was in force.) Marci and Uncle Jenő had exemption documents. Incidentally, János had served three and a half years at the front, Marci not even a single day. The entire incident imparted the injustice of some wild and nonsensical crap game. The lieutenant of the gendarmes did not accept water and wine from me. The troops sat down with the Frenchmen. (What could they talk about and how?)

I cannot describe the horrible fear and despair that overcame me. I thought for a little while, then decided to speak to the lieutenant, and whatever the price, to persuade him with entreaty and bribery not to take János away. He constantly avoided me, however. And I could not say anything in the presence of anyone else, because then it would be impossible *ab ovo* for him to keep the matter to himself.

I was trembling inside, while displaying a strange, icy calm at the same time. János shrugged his shoulders and said, "Well, dear God, if this is the way it has to be..." According to him, you could not negotiate with the army, you could not ask anything from it. I pretended I had changed my mind.

The time for the troops' departure approached. They were packing up and saddling their horses. Then the lieutenant unexpectedly entered the room on the left, where I was alone. Maybe I was even expecting him. He immediately wanted to retreat. "You did not want to meet with me," I said, offering him a place to sit. "No," he said, waving his hand. He sat down grudgingly.

I did not say a single word about János. I did not request anything. I looked at him and asked if he had a wife. I asked about his mother and sisters. But he understood my unexpressed request perfectly. I also knew – without a word being exchanged about it – that they would not take János away. All this took but a few minutes.

They were already departing. Everyone was terrified. Were they going to take him away or execute him on the spot? I made a sign to János that everything was all right.

Afterwards, everyone plied me with questions about what I had done to persuade the lieutenant; they did not quite believe that we hadn't spoken about anything. I think my unspoken entreaty had an effect. By the way, if I had expressed it, he would have been playing with own his life. The Szálasi government was in power.

Later on, I also sensed this, that pleading, weeping, making a scene never helped. There was already enough of this in the war for everyone. The unspoken entreaty was far more effective. But, of course, you do have to back it up with your courage and will power stretched to its limits. At the time, I did not think of such things, I was not aware of all this; I had really prepared myself for the opposite. During such intense moments, something I cannot describe guides me with absolute certainty, something that dwells both inside and outside me.

The Russians finally reached the foot of the mountain. The foresters brought us the news. We were just getting ready for Christmas. Marci, Uncle Jenő, and Katinka packed up and moved on. They urged us to go with them. You know how the reasoning goes. We entrusted our two beautiful Kádár paintings and our Thorma painting[23] to their care (which Miklós and I then presented to Kálmán Tompa at a later date).[24] To their credit, they returned them to us a year later. They were going to Vértesnána. János went to fetch Mami; she had to help the Esterházys wind up the manor's affairs. All were beside themselves and tried to dissuade him, saying that he would run directly into the arms of the Russians. But he started off. "I promised her I would, so I am going for her." He was extremely honorable and brave in such matters. I was in despair; I feared for him, but I couldn't tell him not to go after his mother; and he wouldn't let me go with him.

He headed out in a light buggy. At the time, he had grown a full Jesus-Christ beard, and wore a mackinaw and boots. (I also had a pair of small, light boots made of Halina cloth. He had brought the material from Italy; it was not possible to navigate the mountains otherwise.) Outdoors was a winter morning, glittering snow and dazzling sun. The day wore to a close. Next, a day of anxious waiting. I looked outside, inside intently. They returned. At the foot of the mountain they had encountered only Hungarian and German bands that were escaping, retreating in disorder. The Russians had not yet reached Csákvár.

Mami was pleasant, calm, and hard of hearing when she arrived. She said little. She brought a sack with her. "This is a Christmas gift for you and János," she said. It contained ten bolts of fine bed linen. I had never seen so many in my whole life.[25] (I did not use ten centimeters of the material. The Russians cut it up for footcloths. With it, a whole outfit provided themselves with footcloths.)

We prepared for Christmas. Now that Marci and Katinka had left, only Mami, János, and I occupied the room. I rearranged everything, scrubbed and cleaned up the place thoroughly, and put carpets on the floor. I also improvised a little writing table in front of a window sill for János, so he could work and write, if he so wished. (The Frenchmen helped me to scrub the floor, but it didn't seem to work. Finally, it became clear that they did it more simply: they poured the hot water on the floor, then they wiped it up with a scrubbing cloth, and it was done. We, on the other hand, did the cleaning from a bucket; namely, after gathering up the hot water, we rinsed the floor with cold water. They had never heard of this before. We marveled at each other, mutually.)

Besides the enamel plaque, we carried with us a papal yellow flag and also a red flag, which was hidden. János also received a certificate that designated him as a nunciature (papal legation) official. According to plans, Angelo Rotta, papal nuncio at the time, was preparing to escape to Csákvár if the Germans did not surrender Budapest. At Bicske, he supposedly crawled under his car when the road came under attack. Nothing more was known about him.

We waited for the Russians or the English with growing impatience. We were defenseless; we could be wiped out at any moment by the partisans, the Germans, the gendarmes, or even the Hungarian soldiers. But no. Not the soldiers. Their officers, maybe – acting on command. No one on the German side still believed in victory. And yet, court martials were being held, and executions by firing squad were carried out. According to the massacre decree in force at the time, anyone could be stood against the wall. No one knew what and whom anyone feared. Despite this, we somehow trusted each other; strangers did, too. Orders were greater in number than deeds.

In this connection, the following joke comes to my mind. In Munich, a man asks another, "Tell me, do you think the Führer will be victorious?" The one asked looks around cautiously, pulls his friend under a gate; he looks around again, makes a sign, leads him to the end of the yard, sees a haystack; they crawl into it; there he leans toward his friend's ear and whispers, "Yes, I do." When I think back on it now, there was some talk about new secret weapons. What would have happened if the Germans had had the atomic bomb at their disposal? I know that Hungary was not on the list of *Dienstvolk* (a people of menials) but on the list of expendables. This was how Hitler classified peoples. How could the Jewish people have become victims to it? And the German people, how did they turn into murderers? And we still have not recovered from our surprise that Stalinism imitated fascism, exterminating millions in the name of class warfare. How could the Russian people and so many peoples of the world have become victims to this?

In my view, there is no answer, save one, "Lord, have mercy on us!"

Nyunyuka suddenly went berserk because Marci and his wife had left, and Mami had arrived. Maybe she was in such high spirits because only Mami and I were in the room (the men had gone hunting again). She began springing about, and practically danced. She jumped over the furniture with enormous leaps and kept throwing herself into the air. Mami and I watched her, laughing. I was just about to hand out various things for the holiday and to see how far along our "chefs" were, what they were doing, when we heard the sound of a car horn. We were very surprised, for, according to our understanding, no car had ever been able to make it up to the lodge. It was difficult enough with horses and a wagon. We ran outside. Two German military vehicles were standing in front of the lodge. One looked like a truck, but was something else. Three officers jumped out; I saw the heads of several more soldiers. Meanwhile, they did not shut off their motors. They walked quickly over to us and ordered us to get into the vehicle immediately because the Russians would be arriving within an hour or two. The gendarmes had left our lodge to hunt for partisans (actually they had only warmed themselves up at our place), and the Russians would shoot every one of us in reprisal and reduce the house to ashes.

Mami turned so pale she could barely translate the German, and she broke into silent tears. "The men are not here," I replied. "We cannot leave until they come back." "They are not coming back," they declared flatly. "I am not leaving," I said. "Then I am not, either," Mami added.

I asked the others what they wanted to do. I ran toward the interior. Naturally, they did not want to leave. It would have been somewhat difficult for them, given the fact that they were Jewish, to accept this unusual German rescue.

Efforts at persuasion followed quickly, but I just shook my head. *"Ich kann nicht deutsch sprechen und ich gehe nicht."*[26]

Then they inquired about weapons. "Gladly," I replied, and gave them every weapon in the house very willingly and happily, from the expensive Belgian sporting gun to the Russian machine gun, all the cartridges and cleaning rods and, of course, the hand grenades. I was quite shocked when two soldiers carried out the cartridges; I had thrown them into a wood basket, and it was half full.

I especially hated the hand grenades, in part because of the accident that befell the three boys, in part because of an adventure that had a fortunate outcome. One day the gendarmes were present just as Marci ran into the room, whipped off his shirt, and said, "Don't be angry. I have to take off my shirt; quickly take out the splinters from my back." I removed twelve slivers. One of the gendarmes was wounded in the face; they bandaged that themselves. Someone else among us was also wounded in the head, but I do not remember who it was. My hands shook so badly as I performed my duty that Uncle Jenő had to help me. They reassured me that János was all right, but I did not believe them. If that was the case, then where was he?

What had happened was that they were curious about how the Soviet hand grenade worked – they had just then obtained them from the partisans; they broke one open and the percussion cap ignited. It blew the top of the table apart. They quickly fell on their faces. That was how Marci's back caught the splinters. Three still untouched hand grenades remained on the table; if those had also exploded, not one of those in the room would have remained among the living.

In short, I handed the firearms over happily, and the Germans stowed them away quickly. One of the officers held out his hand. When I accepted it, he swiftly jerked my arm and pulled me up into the vehicle. I began scuffling savagely, broke loose, and leaped from the moving vehicle. I fell headlong, of course, but I jumped to my feet and threatened them.

To this day, the scene makes me laugh. Really, who was I threatening on the car loaded with two soldiers and all those weapons? (I had a similar feeling on another occasion. After the revolution of '56, a military vehicle was coming toward me from the opposite direction, a light machine gun mounted in front and about twenty soldiers with machine guns thrust out on both sides. They were dashing along. They were carrying two flags, one with national colors, the other a red one, and they were singing, *"Spin the silk, comrade."*[27] I became so acutely infuriated that I thought I would stand in front of the vehicle, because then they would stop and I would slap their faces.)

However, if the Germans had really wanted to, they could have taken me away. I wonder, though, why did they want us to go with them? Why did they pull me into the vehicle? I pondered this a lot. If they wanted to ransack the lodges, they could have done that. If we resisted, they could have shot us all with the Russian machine guns I gave them, and they could have put the blame on the partisans if anyone at all would have asked them. Possibly, they were truly sorry for me and wanted to save me.

At last, our men returned. What great joy and happiness! "The dirty Germans," and such. I gave them the weapons? They almost tore me to pieces, they became so infuriated. What will we do now without weapons? What will become of us now? (I was glad we were rid of the weapons, but I did not say anything.) By the way, a small pistol remained in the pocket of one of the Frenchmen. However, he kept quiet about it.

I went about decorating the Christmas tree. We were just lighting the candles when fleeing Hungarian soldiers knocked on the door. We welcomed everyone. This was János's maxim. (Mine, too.) How could we possibly send anyone back into the wintry cold empty-handed? We quickly dressed them in civilian clothing. We threw their uniforms under the manure pile one by one. I gave each of them a Christmas present, chocolates, cigarettes, a pencil, a holiday supper, wine. Those poor grateful, tearful men.

This was the kind of Christmas Eve it was. Moved, we celebrated the birth of Jesus, and waited for the Redeemer, snowy woods and sixteen dogs around us. Each dog got a hunk of deer sausage. Naturally, we drank. Everyone embraced and kissed me; we went back to our room like that. Mami tucked me in and kissed me again. János didn't say a single word. After the light was turned off, I waited and kept listening.

In vain! He didn't come or speak to me. I crawled in beside him. "Go back," he said, "Mami will hear us." Suddenly a violent trembling overcame me, like a fit of shivering. I slipped back to my mattress without saying a word.

I had trouble sleeping. The next day, I awoke with a very heavy heart. The first day of Christmas! It was always my most joyful family holiday. Pure brilliance, splendor, mirth. (I had several brothers and sisters.) I found it very hard to restrain myself. We breakfasted. Not a single word broke the silence.

That morning is sharply engraved in my mind. I was wearing a red, matelassé floor-length dressing gown with the holiday in mind. I was spreading honey on the bread and looking out at the falling snow. It was coming down heavily, in large flakes. I saw the figures of two snow-covered horsemen in the yard in camouflaged, hooded overcoats. Like an apparition!

They looked completely different from Hungarian or German soldiers. Maybe it was because of their snow-covered round hoods and the red star on the front of their fur caps, but also because of their faces. "The Russians," I shouted, jumping up and pointing outside. Förstner and two Frenchmen sprang in from the other room.

The next minute, the Russians kicked the door in with their boots. A soldier, covered with snow, stopped in the doorway, his machine gun raised to fire. He pointed it at each of us, one after the other, without making a single sound. I never looked at the gun barrel, but always at the person he was aiming at. Everyone's face changed, the eyes of one widening, the another's narrowing. And I noticed other things as well. (I had many opportunities after this to observe the play of this fear on faces.)

After the startled, mute silence, the soldier asked something in Russian. We did not understand him.

Förstner, frightened but in impeccable German, began to explain that we were members of a diplomatic corps and so on. He turned extremely pale. I became frightened. What is this blockhead explaining in German? I interrupted him. "*Vengerski,*" I said, pointing at ourselves. "*Jevreji,*" pointing at Förstner. "*Ruski soldat dobre. Nyemecki ne dobre*."[28] At this, they became friendlier. They put us into a corner. They asked if we

89

had any weapons. "No." More soldiers rushed in and started to search the place. They turned the lodge upside down in minutes; they pulled and scattered everything all over the place; they went through everything from one end to another. They found the pistol in the Frenchman's pocket. "What are you doing with that?" "You will die for this." I now saw fear on the Frenchman's face. That certain kind of fear. These troops had fought their way through Rumania; they knew a little Rumanian. We quickly discovered this, and I began to do the interpreting. (I also told them who we were; it was of no interest to them.)

They hadn't even taken the Frenchman away, when they brought in one of the Hungarian soldiers we had welcomed the previous night. They had found something in his pocket that resembled a certificate. I do not know what it could have been, I wasn't able to look it over. I didn't have to translate it because the tall, fine figure of a man, with a good Hungarian face, suddenly began speaking Russian fluently. He was very tense, however. You could tell they were accusing him of something. He was struggling bitterly, but it seemed he was unable to set up a defense for himself. They led him away. There were three short, staccato racks from behind the lodge. When I looked questioningly at János, he signaled that they had just killed him. Then they took the Frenchman. (He turned up the next day, pale and broken.)

All this transpired extremely fast. Afterwards, they simply did not bother with us any more. They looked upon us as neutral objects. We, however, tottered and stumbled around among them; after all, there were thirty to forty persons to a room. It was impossible to move about. Everyone wanted to get warm. The stable filled up in seconds, and the horses stood in a circle under the trees, covered with jackets, greatcoats, carpets, and of course, also with our quilted coverlets. They laid their hands on everything as if unaware that it did not belong to them. If we were standing or sitting somewhere, they let us alone, provided they did not exactly want that exact spot. Whenever they did, they simply pushed us aside with the utmost indifference. At night, we crouched in a corner and slept three to a mattress. In a curious way they had respect for this. If they did sometimes sit on the edge of a mattress, rarely did one of them lie down on it.

One time, on one of the first nights, Mina came in and said, "Just imagine, they brought in a side of one of our stags, they cut the whole thing into pieces. Two soldiers ground up the meat. (We had two meat grinders). A third rubbed the floor with a little snow and began kneading the meat right then and there on the floor. He rolled up his shirt sleeves; his hands were black to his wrist, white above it." (This reminds me that I saw them do many things, but I never saw any of them wash up, not a single Russian soldier. Except a woman. I shall write more about her later. Many washed their feet, though, before wrapping them in the new footcloths they had ripped from the bed linens.)

They prepared the meat in the following way. They salted it, added garlic, and seasoned it with bay leaves. Then they fried the big dumpling-shaped pieces of meat in lard. Naturally, our precious frozen meat was as nothing for so many men. Yes, they had to have something else to eat. Whatever they could find. I saw neither a camp kitchen nor a bag of food with them. In a curious way, unlike Hungarian and German soldiers, they never carried anything other than their weapons with them. (Except for their loot.) They carried a knife in the tops of their boots. They simply had no knapsack or kit bag. They didn't need blankets, because they could lie down in the snow in their wadded, quilted clothing and fur-lined jackets.

The evening of that same day, the officers invited us to their table to eat with them.[29] They put three ominous-sized meat dumplings on my plate. They also offered some to Mami, but she became ill and went outside to vomit. After a little hesitation, I ate half and offered the rest to János, but he didn't want to take it. Frankly speaking, they didn't taste bad. After supper, I hurriedly looked for Mina and told her I had eaten some of the minced meat. We laughed so hard that the soldiers eyed us suspiciously from head to foot, wondering what our problem was. János became angry with us. Actually, it never occurred to me for a moment that among so many men, one of them would look upon me as a woman; I moved among them completely without apprehension and, to the extent circumstances permitted, without prejudice. Mina, Marianne, and Klári did so, too.

Mami and Nyunyuka retired into their shells; they became mentally ill. Nyunyuka lost interest in the dogs.

Actually, it is very difficult for me to relate what the situation was like. There was never any tranquility and stillness. In the lodge we were like passengers on a packed streetcar. Some of us slept at night, some during the day sitting on the floor, leaning against one another. We never really slept.

The soldiers came and went night and day. The units also replaced each other. The days blurred into a strange, fog-like, oppressive dream.

The well ran dry. The Russians cooked with melted snow. First they watered the horses, rather than drink themselves. Of course, we also suffered everything with them. We hadn't washed ourselves for a long time. There was no place, water, or opportunity to do so. We ate what they ate. We were always only dozing even when we slept. Quarrels broke out, sometimes there was shouting.

More and more soldiers came. Some were rough. We waited every day for them to leave and we would be rid of them. One time, the lodge unexpectedly became empty again. I cleaned up the place and we settled back in Then the Rumanian soldiers came. When I spoke to them in Rumanian, weeping, they threw themselves upon me and kissed my hand. They had lost heart among so many savages, fighting the Hungarians and the Germans.

They begged for a little food. The fact that I gave them only some crusts of bread still troubles my soul today. Weeping, they thanked me for that, too. We were running out of everything, and I did not dare take out what we had stowed away.

At the beginning of our time there, we hid a can of lard in the ground in the woods near the cliffs. This was our final cache. Several times, I prepared to go back and find it during times of starvation late in the war, then in peacetime. (This experience later became the theme of Miklós's drama entitled *Bunker*.)

We yearned for peace more than I can say. (Not so the Russians; they wanted Berlin. They were the victors, they were enjoying the war.)

The soldiers taught us Russian in an extremely simple way. One morning when I looked out the window, they said,

"*Zima*." I looked at them uncomprehendingly. At this, one of the soldiers grabbed me, took me out, pressed a big bunch of snow against my neck, and said, "*Zima! Rozhume?*" I understood, and since then, I know it means cold. Or snow? No matter, to me "*zima*" means snow pressed against my neck, and it is cold.

One time they brought out some kind of liquor, poured it into a tumbler, and said we were drinking to Stalin's health, and the one who did not toss it down was a traitor. I don't know how I understood what they said. I think I learned Russian very quickly. Besides, they knew a few words of Rumanian as well.

We stood in a circle, I remember. I raised the tumbler to my lips and sensed it contained brandy. I wanted to stop, but they yelled at me, and I had to drain it. To me a water glass of brandy meant intoxication. János took hold of me, led me to a corner, sat me down, and squatting, crouching, I quickly fell asleep. By the time I awoke I had sobered up, after a fashion. They had not harmed me. It never entered my mind that they would.

I had seen those posters in Budapest showing a Soviet soldier ripping a crucifix from a woman's neck. I heard they ravished women. I also read leaflets reporting the Russians did this and that. I didn't believe any of it; it was all German propaganda, I thought. I found it unimaginable that they would knock women down, that they would break their backs, and commit other horrors. Then I learned how their backs were broken. Very simply, unintentionally.

One day one of the soldiers took the Yugoslav priest's watch It was an old, large-shaped pocket watch with Roman numerals that the priest greatly treasured. He complained to me about it. I think he spoke in German; I understood him.

I became horribly infuriated. I went in and asked him to point out the soldier who had taken it; I stood in front of the soldier, and scolding him loudly, I demanded he return the watch. The others stood there, the soldiers; they watched and listened to the scene; they did not say a word.

Actually, it was quite easy to communicate with the Russians. It was also possible to shout at them in Hungarian. I had known for a long time that the more primeval and primitive, the nearer to nature a people are, the more they understand what someone is saying if his gestures are appropriate. They comprehend correctly what we also call metacommunication from the tone, the mimicking, the emphasis. They returned the watch to the priest. Dear God, how naive I was then. I did not know there was reason to be afraid.

I also explained to them that we were members of the diplomatic corps, extra-territorial and immune. They took these words literally; they surrounded me, laughed, repeatedly slapped me in the face, hit me (not very hard). "There, you see, you are not immune." Another time, they demanded I step "outside the territory." They watched curiously, to see how I would do it.

This was not a joke. They thought that immunity was some type of merciful force; it would, for example, stop dead in mid-air the hand of anyone trying to hit you. Or they did not believe it at all. They were atheists, with a few exceptions, and, to my consternation, anti-Semites. When they derided Förstner for being a Jew, I upbraided them indignantly, and they stopped immediately.

Of course, the horses stayed outdoors during the nights, because there was not enough room in the stable; I don't know why they didn't freeze to death. Nor do I exactly know what happened to the sixteen dogs. In any case, many of them died, but three of them were always around me, Filike, Milkó – the name of the third one is always on the tip of my tongue, but I don't, can't come up with it.

I often thought I should just keep on trying various names. The moment comes to my mind when some weeks later, this dog saw me on a street in Csákvár, dashed toward me, and was run over by a car. It darted along joyfully, and I cried out its name. I should shout that name now, too, but I simply can't get it out.

It was intrinsically strange that the Russians did not kick the three dogs out of the house; instead, they let them stay and huddle there, to lie beside me, on my legs, arms, and shoulders; there was really no room for them. I do not remember what Nyunyuka did in those days.

There was also a woman in the detachment. Nadya was her name. One night she grabbed me by the wrist and led me into the kitchen; we locked the door somehow – I believe we tied it with a piece of twine. She shouted something in Russian; I think it was "leave us alone." She heated some water, washed her hair, and bathed; she washed out her brassiere and panties and immediately put them back on, wet. First, she asked me, when she was undressing, to cut through the twine that tied her brassiere together in back, the only way she could slip out of it. Next she asked me to wash her back, and then, when she put on her still wet brassiere again, to tie it together with twine. "Good and tight!" she urged me, to keep pulling. I was flabbergasted. Then I understood that she would be engaged in battle for weeks like this; only by being bound up so rigidly, so tightly, could she move about and ride a horse among so many men – she was a cavalryman, in male clothing.

But I did not understand why one woman would be assigned to be with men. I never saw them teasing or hugging her. There was also a child with them, or a young boy who could still be called a child; he was also a soldier and engaged in battle with them. The soldiers romped and played pranks on him a lot. He was a very sweet boy; occasionally he played with me, just like a boy-child.

Then another detachment of soldiers arrived that ate raw meat. It was icy meat, freshly cut pork, plainly frozen raw, because it had frozen in a sack thrown on a horse in the cold. I don't know who they were; they didn't speak Russian. They offered me some; we ate it salted; it wasn't bad.

In our room hung an old-style wooden telephone apparatus, installed on the wall; it linked the residents of the forest lodges with one another and the central office of the forestry – it had stopped functioning a long time ago. I heard them as one said to another, "Nye robota."[30] One time, when a new unit arrived and they lifted the receiver, I said, "Nye robota." At this, they dashed up to me, they wanted to slap me in the face, they tugged away at me. They took me for a spy. If I knew Russian, then how come I did not know it, and if I did not know it, then how come I did know it. This was how we lived.

One lovely morning, they suddenly packed up all of us, provided us with a wagon on which we could load some of our belongings. Mami could have got into it, but she did not want to; she preferred to come with us. The rest (us) they herded down the hill on foot with a little slip of paper in our hands. Something was written in Cyrillic letters on a slip of paper the size of a palm torn from a square notebook; we were unable to read it. A Russian soldier escorted us, on horseback naturally; we went on foot. When we arrived in Pusztakő-hányás, they turned us over to a larger unit. A pair of mounted soldiers rode in front, after them a good many men and women on foot, and in the rear, more mounted soldiers. We continued on this way, I do not know to where. There, another detachment joined us. They then separated the women and the men. János and I looked at each other: they must be pushing us on into a prisoner-of-war camp. We thought of Siberia, all the more because it was midwinter, the snow was hard, the sun glittered, there was a heavy frost. We went on, dragging ourselves along in the band, on an unknown road.

I was cut off from János. No one did much talking. We were a fairly large group. Those who couldn't bear it dropped in their tracks; the soldiers kicked or shot them. It was mostly the elderly, women, and children who collapsed from fatigue; they would not have been able to go any farther anyway; they would have frozen to death quickly if a bullet had not finished them off. One thing is certain. I did not know we were crossing the firing line.

We moved along like this until nightfall. Mami was already having trouble walking. We held her on each side and trudged along. The poor dear dragged her legs, her tears flowed.

My heart began to ache badly – it is a poor way to express it, but I have no other way of putting it. Then I was seized by a savage rage and fury against the Russians, the kind of rage and fury I rarely ever feel in my life. At times like this, I am overcome by such audacity that I am not afraid of anything in the world.

I jumped out of the line; I don't know why they didn't shoot me. I ran forward and grabbed the bridle of the horse of the soldier leading the group. By then I had long stopped fearing horses; they are better than human beings. The horse stopped dead and reared as I dug in my heels. The horseman raised his whip and dealt me a blow, or wanted to; I no longer remember, it is not very important.

The fact is, I shouted a word or two in Russian and in Hungarian, "Beasts! Don't you see the women and children can't take it?" I yelled, "*Stoj*! Stop!" And we stopped! The soldiers and the entire band, everyone sank down where they were standing and tried to rest a little and pee. I don't know how long we paused there; then we dragged ourselves to our feet and plodded on. After that, my memory disintegrated from fatigue and cold; I do not know what happened.

Suddenly, I was standing all alone in a small, clean, friendly cottage. It consisted of a single room; a fire was burning in the stove, it gave off light. It may have been a hunting lodge or a guardroom.

To my great surprise, a man in a German officer's uniform was sitting there, his legs bandaged or covered with a cast; he was speaking to a Russian officer of higher rank standing beside him. I showed him the slip of paper and tried to explain it was a "*diplomathiicheski corpus,*" and I tried to explain in Russian, Hungarian, Rumanian, and German that they should let us go, that what they were doing was illegal, inhuman.

The officer looked at me attentively, summoned a soldier – I no longer know from where – and ordered him to single us out and let us go free. They released the French prisoners of war, the Yugoslav priest, the delegate of the nunciature, his mother, Klári, the little girl, Mina, her mother, János, Mami, and me to go wherever we wanted.

Before they released us, they returned the slip of paper and gave each of us a slice of bread, altogether a half loaf of bread. We hadn't eaten since breakfast, though I don't remember whether we had eaten at all in the morning. I put my slice of bread into my coat pocket, so that later, when I would be very hungry, I would eat it, or if anyone could no longer bear it, I would give it to him. With that, we set out, knowing – because they had informed us – that we were in the front line of the battle.

We headed out blindly. According to János, we were not far from Csákvár; he was familiar with the road leading there. First, we had to take a shortcut through some woods. What was strange here – it was already growing dark – was that I continually saw projectiles flying. I literally saw them; they were colorful, they gave off a green light. "Tracer projectiles," said János. Years later, on the dawn of November 4, 1956, when Miklós observed colorful projectiles from the window, he said that the Russian attack was about to begin, they were "tracer projectiles". And the assault did commence.

We reached the outskirts of Csákvár at night. A patrol had already been posted: a Russian soldier was walking back and forth on a straight line.

The dogs, too, had rejoined us. The three dogs still alive followed us faithfully. While we were with the band, they followed us from afar, at a distance, so the soldiers would not notice them – they would have shot them. They knew many things, they were hunting dogs. This was their good fortune, and also ours, because we might have had to pay for them with our lives.

We trudged with great difficulty through the woods in the deep snow between thickets, and reached the trail leading to the village. We were dead tired. János did not allow us to rest; he believed we would not be able to get up, having dragged ourselves along since morning.

Night falls early in winter, but to us it seemed as if that night would never end. In fact, it was moonlit, and the snow added light to the scene. We remained quiet at the edge of the woods; then we lay down on our stomachs. We were able to calculate exactly that, as the guard walked forward, he would reach the point where we were located and then turn around and head in the opposite direction-his back was now turned to us! While his back was to us, we could creep ahead across the road. On the other side was a ditch – like depression, and we could press on in this depression. When the guard turned around – we had to figure this out – we would have to wait in the depression, mute, lying on our stomachs. When he walked past, and his back was to us again, we could creep on, then lie silently again. It was a nerve-racking game. János knew how to play it; he had covered this road five times before. He always gave the signal for us to drop to our stomachs and not to move on – then to move on. If someone missed a movement, it would be over for all of us. He knew for certain that on the firing line they would shoot without asking a question. And if they did ask, what could we have said?

Was it for this that the Russians had evacuated us?[31] Was it for this that those who fell out of the line had to die? And as for why they released us, I have no idea whatsoever. Though we were carrying the document identifying us as members of a diplomatic corps and so on, in the end they had let us go into the firing line: on that night no identity check would have been conducted there. We were left for the last, János, Mami, I, and the dogs. János took Mami across. Then I followed with the dogs. He was very angry about the dogs. He swore at me very softly, firmly, whispering: It was my lunacy, the dogs should have been shot, they should have been tied to a tree. They have to be killed!

I did not want to kill them. I myself did not want to live very much. However, I wanted the others to live, particularly János and Mami. I heard him out, and then we started off again, crawling, he in front, I after him, with Filike right beside me. The other two dogs were in the rear. They knew how to comply with János's commands more promptly than I or anyone else did. When the signal came to lie on our stomachs in silence, they did not budge. When we crawled on our stomachs, they did, too. When we remained motionless, they did, too. They did not make a single sound. They remained perfectly mute.

Good Lord! the intelligence, obedience, faithfulness of these dogs! It was easier to crawl with them and me than with the others, János told me subsequently.

At the end of the ditch stood a hut resembling a presshouse without a cellar. Its door was broken in. We crawled in silently one by one on our stomachs, mutely, as before; then János restored the door, putting something in front of it. Inside were two bunks, just bare boards. We lay prostrate on the ground and the bunks. Exhausted, we fell asleep. We did not feel cold, because there were so many of us in the little place.

Hammering on the door about dawn. Now we were done for! The dogs began barking. János jumped to the door. They were Russian soldiers with a Hungarian man in tow. The Hungarian recognized János; he said something to the soldiers. Probably he said he "belongs here," he "lives here," he is "innocent," or God knows what. They did not rough him up.

I wanted to take out my slice of bread in the morning but found only crumbs in my pocket. It had crumbled.

Then we headed away from the house-like structure amid horrible anxieties; we were nearing Csákvár. We reached it by noon. Now, too, brilliant sunshine, a hard, cold winter, and glittering snow surrounded us.

I remember, the old lady, Förstner's mother – I have forgotten her name – became very optimistic: she wanted to go to the hairdresser. We would have our hair done and then have lunch prepared for us, she said. I called her attention, somewhat exasperatedly, to the fact that we were in a battle area, at the front. She looked at me, astonished, "The hairdresser can still work." "But there isn't one in Csákvár, anyway," I said.

I do not know how we wound up at the parsonage; this has already become muddled in my mind. The fact is that we were there and had been directed there,[32] and, wonder of wonders, the wagon arrived from the forester's lodge with all of our belongings. So, as I put it, nothing in the whole world had disappeared. The Russians unorganized organization remains an eternal mystery to me. The same is true of their behavior; you could never figure out anything they did. Anything and the opposite of anything could happen. There was Nyunyuka in the traveling basket. A very long time had passed, almost two days. We took her out. She squatted and began to pee; she peed and peed interminably. Cats are so clean, she could bear the day and a half in the basket without messing it. (One of the basic problems of the war was that you had to void – yes, but when and where; oddly, even when you have not eaten for days. Later, I experienced this also with the comatose who were dying.)

We settled into the parsonage. Living there were the minister, who was an archdeacon at the same time, his chaplain, and the rest of us. It was quite a large residence, an L-shaped building, the kitchen in the back. The French prisoners of war again lived in the kitchen and did the cooking. A glassed-in veranda stretched all the way to the large yard. Windows overlooked the front garden toward the square.

A guard, a Soviet soldier, stood in front of the entrance; he did not let anyone enter. The village was bombed occasionally, but we supposedly led a peaceful existence. Except the clergymen. They behaved abominably. I remember, the Yugoslav priest was lying on a bed in the chaplain's room. He was ill, old, and deaf. One time, I took something out of the chaplain's cabinet, a glass or something, to give the priest a drink and forgot to put it back. For this, the chaplain rebuked me severely, sharply, as if I wanted to steal the glass. I don't know what else occurred, but this I do, that I would have liked to slap his face. Up to that point in my life I would never have struck a human being or an animal. I said to him, "Sir, listen to me. I have never slapped anyone in the face in my whole life, but now, if I did not take into consideration that you are a minister, I would definitely slap your face."

The archdeacon had us beat the dust out of his Persian carpet; he tried to hide his possessions and made excuses for them, but he did not so much as give us a piece of potato, though his potato supply stood three to four meters deep in one half of his cellar, a large, four-cornered area. Then, during the course of battles, it was spread about and covered the entire area one meter deep. Meanwhile, Csákvár was being shelled. "Tell me, archdeacon, do you fear God?" I asked him. He looked at me and said, "It is quite clear you are a Protestant. You speak impudently with priests." (He was tall, with a small, bulging paunch, always dressed in a black frock, and wore a gray hat on his head. His chaplain was gaunt, like someone who ate sparingly.)

One evening the men were playing cards in the cellar, and the women had taken shelter there. János and I stayed upstairs. He was going to take his shoes for repairs in his slippers and lounging jacket. We were sitting on the floor, on the mattress at the foot of the Yugoslav priest's bed, the three dogs beside me. János got up and walked around the narrow room. We listened to the powerful detonations. *"Gott sei dank, heute ist ganz Ruhe,"* [33] the Yugoslav spoke up. He was that deaf. János and I were being amused by this and continuing to crouch at the foot of the bed, so that we would be protected from fragments in case of a hit. The door burst open. Russian soldiers poured in. One grabbed my wrist and jerked me up, the other János. The dogs barked madly, the soldiers shouted.

They laid hold of János and took him outside in his slippers, bareheaded, in his lounging jacket. I ran after him. At the corner I encountered the men coming up from the cellar. The Russians hauled all of them away.

I understood "in the morning" among the words they threw at me. It was horrible. I cannot express what I felt, I simply cannot.

I told Mami and the other women in the cellar that all was quiet upstairs, but that the shelling might begin any minute and so they should stay put and sleep there. The men would defend the house.

Upstairs, I put a pillow across my head to lessen the sound of the explosions; I pressed it against my ears, leaned my forehead against the window, and looked out into the moonlit night. I waited like this for morning to arrive.

I felt with every nerve that now they had really torn János from me, really taken him away, and only God knew what would happen to him. Perhaps I also sensed what lay ahead of us. I believed this was my most abysmal night.

The women came up from the cellar in the morning. There was a stream of complaints and accusations about why I didn't tell them right away what had happened. What could they have done? I replied, curfew was in effect until morning, who would have dared to go outside into the night, and go where and why?

I then set out alone. I tied up my hair with a kerchief and went to the kommandatura. Many others were already sitting there, waiting for their turn. Among them was a young girl whose head was bleeding, a lock of her hair having been ripped out. She was miserable and despondent. "The Russians ran over her," said her mother. I did not understand her. "With a bicycle?" I asked. The woman became furious. "Are you crazy? Don't you know what they do to women?"

I listened to what the people around me were saying: which woman's back broke, which one lost consciousness, which one was bleeding and they could not stop it, a man shot to death for trying to protect his wife.

Suddenly the horror that surrounded us was unfolding. Suddenly it became clear to me that, in the parsonage, next to the Soviet military patrol, acquainted with a few soldiers who were occasionally jovial intruders, looters, and devourers of our food but held in check, we knew next to nothing about what was going on in the outside world. Maybe János did, only he did not tell me about it.

He might have sensed something. Hungarian soldiers could not have behaved any more honorably in the Russian villages. Only, they were not this barbaric. Here the East had invaded the West.

I no longer remember what the commanding officer said to me.

Later, after they released the archdeacon, I learned that the Russians were accusing us of being spies because exactly after the tower clock struck, their headquarters was hit, and many were killed. They thought we had given the signal from the parsonage.

It wasn't possible to explain to them that the tower clock was wound up, that it struck systematically – that this was only sheer coincidence. It was impossible to make the Russians understand many things. They lived in another world, their experiences were different. Their logic was also different. They were not acquainted with tower clocks. Generally it was the watch – they called it *"chasi"* – that they always searched for. I thought that after the Soviet detachments withdrew, there would hardly be a watch left in the entire country.

The minister was very indignant that the Russians had treated him so disrespectfully; they hit him on the head, took away his hat, yelled at him. He said the others had been hauled away and probably put to death.

One day – the minister probably was not even at home at the time, these days are jumbled again – many soldiers came in and went through everything. One of them called me aside and showed me a picture; it was of János in his officer's uniform. Actually, the soldier did not do this so straightforwardly. He showed my picture and pointed at me, indicating "this is you." He asked me about the picture of János dressed as a civilian. "Your husband?" I said yes. Then he produced the one on which we appear together, he in his officer's uniform, and with that, there was nothing more to be said. He shouted in Russian: spy, traitor, officer, German, soldier! How did I understand those words? They were the ones we learned most quickly. And from his countenance.

I had a string bean in my mouth, one from a can, and I felt I could not swallow it, no matter how hard I tried. I moved on and spit it out. The young man shouted: they will shoot him in the head, *"tvoy muzh"* (your man). Then he smiled and called me into the room. I went in with him; I knew what he had in mind. He put the photograph on the nightstand and laid me down on the bed. I was afraid he would not give me the picture. When he was done, he took the picture into his hand and showed it to me again. (I just kept fearing he would not give it to me.) I was wearing a checkered blouse with buttons for closing up and a small pocket. He unbuttoned the blouse, put the photograph inside it, buttoned it up, caressed where the picture lay, then left.

Somehow I put in an appearance. Mami looked at me. I think she knew exactly what had happened, but we did not talk about it.

The following day – the third day – some men we didn't know came from the neighboring village and reported that our men had been executed; they were forced to dig a long ditch and stand at its edge, and then they were shot in the back of the head. Three local inhabitants threw dirt on them. (This is the usual practice, the victims themselves had to dig their own graves – it's the way in every war.)

"It is not true," I told Mami. "I know it is not true." I was terribly frightened and trembling, and I felt inside me that it was not true, or I just wanted to believe it was not true. I did not know exactly how it was, just that it was not true; it was not true, it was not true, I said to myself.

After our men were taken away, it became clear that serious problems existed in the village; the sentry disappeared from the front of the parsonage. (I asked all the women to withdraw into one room and spend the night together; it would be safer that way. But they did not want to because some wanted to bring everything of theirs up from the cellar and keep it next to them; this way, however, we would not have been able to fit into the room.)

I had a small metal box; it was made of a light, fine metal, covered on the outside with colorful paper, like tea canisters today. It contained the gold jewelry I had received as wedding gifts from my great aunt and family; they were lovely Transylvanian goldsmith's work, a hundred to a hundred fifty years old, heavy gold pieces, one or two precious stones, and such. Placed on top were three Chinese porcelain tea cups and saucers that János had given me; he had brought or sent them to me from the Russian front. The china was packed in a soft, straw-like material, and this sat right on top.

A couple of days after our men had disappeared, everyone gathered their things together and began hiding them; they lowered the silver into the well and concealed the more valuable objects under the manure pile, and the jewels in their beds, and so on. I pushed this box under the Yugoslav priest's bed; I visited him frequently to feed and attend to him.

Since the women did not want to stay in one room, we dispersed. It was growing dark. I was sitting with Mami in our room, afraid. It was quiet, a fire was burning in the tile stove, there was no shelling going on at the time.

Three Russians came in; they told me in Rumanian to go with them. I knew exactly what they wanted; I don't know how, but I knew.

I told Mami they were taking me to the hospital to take care of the casualties. Mami looked at me and pleaded with me, saying, "Don't go, dear girl, don't go. Don't go with them, they will do something bad with you." I told them my mother would not let me (I did not want to say "mother-in-law). They pointed to the corner of the stove door, which was reinforced with iron, and said they would bash Mami's head against it if I did not go with them. (When I close my eyes, I can still see that stove door.) They said this in Rumanian. I said to Mami in Hungarian that casualties were heavy, I had to go.

I put on my boots and tied my hair in a kerchief. Then I untied and tied it again, untied it and tied it again to gain time. As I was standing, I heard something thumping on the floor. It was the heels of my boots, I was trembling so hard.

I hugged and kissed Mami. "I will stay only as long as I have to help," I said to her. "Think of the wounded." Mami looked at me and began crying.

We went out to the L-shaped corridor. (It was there in the middle of the L-shape that the Russians had encountered our men when they took them away.) Arriving in the middle of the

"L," I attacked them wildly without saying a word. I kicked and hit them with all my strength, but in the next moment I was on the floor. No one emitted a sound, not they, nor I; we tussled mutely. They took me back to the kitchen and threw me to the ground – apparently I was trying to defend myself or attack them – and my head struck the corner of the trash can. It was made of hardwood, as befitted an archdeacon's residence. I lost consciousness.

I regained consciousness in the archdeacon's large inner bedroom. The panes were broken, the windows boarded up; nothing was on the bed but bare boards; I was lying on it. One of the Russians was on top of me. I heard a woman's voice ricocheting from the ceiling, "Mommy, Mommy!" it shouted. Then I realized it was my voice, that I was shouting.

When I realized this, I stopped; I lay quiet, motionless. My physical feeling had not returned with my consciousness; it was as if I had become petrified with fear or grown cold. I had reason to feel cold in that windowless, unheated room with the lower part of my body naked. I do not know how many Russians worked me over or how many of them had before. When day began to dawn, they left me there. I got up, I could move only with great effort. My head, my entire body ached. I was bleeding profusely. I did not feel that they had raped me but that they had attacked me physically. This had nothing to do with embraces or sex. It had nothing to do with anything. It was simply – I just now realize, as I am writing, that the word is accurate: aggression. That is what it was.

I do not know whether it was then or some other time, but the Russians took everyone away. Mami, too. It was bearable for me; after all, I was already a woman, but Mina was just a girl. I went through the house and tracked her down by following her weeping and whimpering; she was lying stretched out on the cement floor in a chamber-like room. I went to her. "Let's not go out to the left," she said. "There are still some Russians there and they will attack us again."

We wanted to crawl out into the L-shaped corridor through the window so that we could get back to Mami. I crawled out. Mina would have followed me, but she was chubbier than I and became stuck. I crawled back in through the other section of the narrow triple window and pushed her from behind. They had treated her so roughly that her thighs were covered with wounds. As I pushed her naked bottom – it was stuck in the window – we even laughed. I don't know why we did, but we had to. Outdoors we pulled ourselves together somehow and stole in to Mami. Was it then they took Mami away or some other time? By now, everything is muddled in my head, the nights and days, what happened when? which detachment invaded our privacy when? when were they Russians and when were they Germans? when were we fired upon and when was it quiet? By now, it is not possible for me to know anything for certain. It was not possible then, either.

When they first took me away – I found out later – Mami, crying and shouting, renounced and cursed God. From that day on, she was no longer religious. I became aware much later that she wasn't going to church. Whether she still prayed or not, I don't know. (I now understand why I came across so many atheists in Israel last summer.) I was never able to take Mami to a gynecologist, either, even though they had infected her, they infected all of us. When and who among so many?

On another night, an entire detachment caught us unaware; then they laid us on the ground. It was dark and cold, firing was going on. The following scene remains etched in my mind: Eight to ten Russians on their haunches surround me, first one lies on me, then another. They specified the time allotted to each of them. They looked at a wristwatch; they lit a match from time to time, and one of them had a cigarette lighter; they kept track of the time. They hurried each other. One asked, *"Dobre robota?"* [34]

I didn't move. I thought I would die from it. Of course, you don't die from it. Unless they break your back, but even then, not immediately.

As for how much time passed and how many of them there were, I do not know. Toward dawn I understood why the back broke. They did the following: they pushed the legs toward the shoulders and threw themselves between them on their knees. If one of them did this too hard, the woman's spine would snap, not because they wanted it to, but because of the unrestrained force. They shoved the woman into a curl on a point on her spine backward and forward, and they didn't even notice if it broke. I also believed they would kill me, that

107

I would die in their arms. My back was injured, but it did not break. Because the woman moves on a point at a time like this, my back developed a sore, and my slip and clothing stuck to the wound because it bled, but I did not notice it until later. So many things hurt, I just did not notice it.

(Mina and I often speculated about how many minutes and men there had been during a particular night. They did the very same thing to her in another room. But why always on the floor?)

The village was under fire, there was a constant rattle and grumbling. Then one day, an officer came; he took pity on me, took me into his lap, caressed me, covered me with his coat, and hummed softly to himself. I waited for him to rape me, or possibly he had already done so and had then taken me into his arms, or had taken me from the arms of others. But I do remember clearly that he felt my fingers to see if I was wearing a ring or not. He lit a match and looked. At that moment I removed my ring and handed it to him. My father had worn it on his little finger; real pearls encircled a little green stone in the shape of a horseshoe. It was a woman's ring; that was why he wore it on his little finger. Why did my father like to wear a woman's ring on his little finger?

I don't like rings, so how could I possibly have been wearing one then? Laughing, the officer returned it, reached into his pocket, and pulled out some rings. He kept working them onto my finger, but I did not want one. I smiled and returned each one to him. Perhaps they weren't good rings; by now I no longer know how it came about, just that I didn't want to accept one. Then he released me from his arms and wanted to go out.

Despairing, I ran after him; I held on to the tip of his overcoat and did not let him go. He explained something, I didn't understand him. He went out; I was so afraid I scurried after him. He walked over to the manure pile, stopped, and began to urinate. He looked sideways, saw me, and began laughing.

He came back to me and embraced me again; I made a sign for him to wait. I went to the toilet. I stood on its top, for by then we had not been able to sit down on it for a long time. Up above, in Mindszent, too, in the forester's lodge, the Russians appeared on the scene and did number two not only in it but under, above, beside it, everywhere. It was awful. You had to find a place for your feet so you could stand up. In short, I stood, finished my number one, and then I realized that sometimes you forget to pee because you are afraid or you don't have the time.

I went toward him. He waited for me and took me back to the house; he related many things to me in Russian that I didn't understand. He pulled his fur cap over my head so I wouldn't get cold; when I shivered, he put his quilted jacket on me. We woke to the dawn this way. The night passed better than the others, though I was always afraid he would leave me, and then others would assault me.

As for what happened to Mami and the other women during this time? This episode took place at the beginning. Mina had long hair; a soldier wound it around his hand and dragged her that way. Mina howled and shouted my name. I went to her. "Help me!" she begged. I said to her softly, "Just go." She did; that is, they carried her away.

Did this occur before they took me away, or on only one night or evening, or did it happen again or for the first time then?

The young girl, Marianne, was spared when she began to foam at the mouth and her eyes turned inward. They left her there, but they carried her grandmother off. In the morning, the grandmother told us proudly, "I am disciplined."

We laughed at this.

I went to the doctor I knew in Csákvár; he reassured me that if I bled, I would by no means get any kind of infection. Just the opposite is true, but what could he have done? Nothing.

We were all bleeding and could not wash ourselves. We tried to clean ourselves secretly in the snow.

As to what became of those of us in the parsonage, I don't really remember. The archdeacon just vanished somewhere. I don't think he could bear the fact that Russians carried off his Persian carpets and the silver tableware, and ruined everything. Then the chaplain also disappeared; only we women remained in the parsonage, and the old Yugoslav priest, plus the billeted Russian soldiers.

Sometimes the Russians stole from us, sometimes we helped ourselves to this and that of theirs. Or the other way around: we stole from them and they took this and that from us. The little that remained of our belongings dwindled increasingly. Mamika said to me, "Look here, I rescued this pair of your laced boots. I shall put one of them under the potatoes in the cellar, the other I shall hide behind the mirror." But Mami was mistaken. The one behind the mirror disappeared. We pulled the other boot from under the potatoes to no purpose – you can't walk in one boot.

One time, they wanted to shoot us in the cellar, where we were, by then, living on the top of the potatoes, which had diminished because the Russians were eating them and so were we. I don't know why, but they stood the four of us against the wall, Mami, me, Mina (who was the fourth?) and said they were going to shoot us in the head. The first bullet struck the wall beside me. I turned around and laughed in their faces. When they had stood me against the wall, I felt it wasn't for real; that certain voice inside me told me it was not for real. When the first bullet hit the wall, I knew for certain with my head, my mind that it wasn't. It wasn't possible for a Russian soldier three meters away from the wall to miss his target with a machine gun. They were so surprised when I turned around and laughed that they immediately lowered their weapons. They came over, pounded me on the back, and howled with laughter: Bravo, bravo. They enjoyed it. What? Their joke, my courage, my intuition, their savagery, or the whole comedy?

Of course, they found everything in the well, what we had hidden under the manure pile, what had been buried in the ground. They ferreted with sticks; they dug where the ground was soft and found everything we had stowed away. My box was lying low under the bed. I forgot all about it.

One night I jumped out the window. I don't know whether it was when the house caught fire or some other time, or even why I was fleeing from them: the fact is, I jumped out, barefooted, in just a stitch of clothing, out onto the snow, across the fence, and I was off and running. Filike followed me. The Russians shot at me. They shot neatly around me with their machine guns.

It was a great stunt. That is, it is extraordinarily easy to hit someone with a machine gun; you don't have to aim, just lay down a round in the direction of the target, and a bullet will hit its mark anyway. But to fire around it, that requires skill, to make sure a single bullet does not strike. Now, too, I turned around for an instant, laughing. Meanwhile, I was careful to keep running rhythmically, so they would not hit me accidentally. Filike also maintained the cadence behind me. She was smart, she was good. Filike, Filike! when I think back on this little sandy-colored dog, even now I turn sad and search for her look in every dachshund's eyes. However, if it is better for her not to be living any more, perhaps it is better for everyone.

In short, Filike was running directly behind me; I was careful to run evenly because of her, too, so she would not be shot down. Why was it that I did not want them to hit me? I did not want that mentally. At such a time, you don't think, you just run instinctively; you don't fear death, you feel the whiz of the bullets and would like to elude them.

I was escaping. Nobody wanted to take me in. Everyone was afraid; I was a young, a nineteen-year-old woman, and they knew the Russians often took me away. They were afraid to give me shelter, afraid the Russians would come after me.

Then I begged them to let me into their barn, to let me take shelter beside the cattle. No, no. Let me into the cellar. No. I promised, I vowed I would lie, say I just sneaked in when I saw no one around.

No one wanted to let me through the gate, not even the doctor or any of János's acquaintances that I knew.

I was forced to return to the parsonage, nearly frozen stiff. Filike was beside me. I did not dare go inside, the street at night seemed safer. When I grew extremely cold, I sat down on the steps of the gate leading to the street; Filike lay down there, and I put my legs on her and warmed her up. When my shoulder was freezing, I put Filike on it; when my neck was freezing, I put her there. Filike often protected me from freezing. I wonder, did she know what she was doing or not?

Then on one of those nights when I didn't know who were doing the rampaging, or how, only that it was all unbearable, a section of the house went up in flames. A bomb had struck it. A Russian soldier felt sorry for me, took hold of me, and led me away from there. I called Mami, too; the soldier let me do so. In the winter night, under curfew, we went – the Russian soldier, Mamika, and I – across the square in front of the church. He ushered us into a cellar. (Two years ago, Miklós and I went there; a grocery store stands above it now.) A steep shaft with wooden steps leading down, with a vaulted, small landing, then a wine cellar the size of a hall. Yes, this was it! Sixty to seventy people lay huddled close together in a row on the ground, a narrow passageway in the middle and an even narrower path where they lay two deep on the right. It must have seemed strange to them – those who were awake – that a Russian soldier escorted us in. Only a night lamp was shedding light. They gave Mami a chair; she sat down and stayed there until morning. I could not stand from exhaustion and lay down next to the entrance under the only table in the cellar, the only place where there was a little room. The ground was soaking wet. I pulled my hooded winter coat over my head and fell asleep, rolled into a ball.

Apparently, I had stretched out in my sleep, because when they were waking me up in the morning, someone stepped on my head. They lit some matches. Bending over me, a male voice shouted, "A woman! A young woman!" They asked, "Where did you come from?" "Kolozsvár," "I replied. They started laughing, "Now, directly?" Then I crawled out from under the table, and I said, "No, from the parsonage. " Dead silence enveloped me – apparently they knew what was going on there – but they did not turn me out.

Crazy scenes took place. I remember, they told the town clerk of Gyuró to return to Gyuró, young women dressed in white will greet him there with wreaths and flowers, that's what he deserved. And other things I did not understand. What did I understand? Hand-to-hand fighting for half a meter of space, for a glass of water.

Then Mami and I were given a place in the row where there was room for the two of us beside each other. Someone was so considerate that he helped me remove the front door from a damaged house and haul it to the cellar. The trouble was, it had a protruding iron knob in the center. If we turned it over, there was an iron disk on the other side. Mami and I deliberated for a long time whether we should choose the knob or the disk – for a place to sleep, that is. On one edge of the door was a heavy hinge, on the other a lock, a four-cornered box, a considerably protruding, ancient, primitive door lock with a large latch. Why didn't we try to remove it?

All we had was a pocketknife. In any case, it was very complicated for the two of us to lie on the door, one of us between the knob and the lock, the other between the knob and the hinge. It wasn't exactly soft, either, given that it was constructed of wood and had angular indentations with little frames. In times past, it must have been a beautiful door, but small unfortunately. Mami, on the other hand, was a bit plump and buxom. She struggled to work herself between the latch and knob.

To prevent the Russians from recognizing me, I spread a large black shawl over my shoulders, dirtied my face, and drew wrinkles with coal, and we developed other ruses with the women. I kept Filike under my coat, on my chest; the shawl also covered her. Filike was quiet, she did not yap, she barely snuffled, and when our legs were too cold, then Mami and I looked at each other, and at night, in the dark, we put her on our legs, now warming me, now her. Of course, we were also keeping Filike warm.

What was life like in the cellar? Shelling went on constantly, sometimes incoming, sometimes outgoing. But there was always a cease-fire from six to six-ten in the evening. To this day I don't know why there was a cease-fire or how we knew there would be one. But at that time we would all dash up, women, children, and men; everyone would drop their pants and do their business.

Scenes like these swirled around us, "You idiot, can't you see you are pissing on my foot?" A woman came down, weeping, her high-topped shoe was undone; that was why its shank stood out, and she said, "Just look, I shit in my shoe."

It was twice as hard for me because I had to hold Filike to make sure no one would see her, and she had to pee, too. For this reason I ran farther than the others and took cover behind the pig sty. We finished our business beside each other, together, quaking; we were not afraid of the shelling but of human beings. Sometimes I'd even go up into the firing line, so Filike could pee and I could also relieve myself.

It wasn't easy to do this, but at least I was not witness to degrading scenes. The many naked behinds, all the pissing, shitting, crowding, "Don't bother me! Can't you see?" It was better for Filike and me in the firing line, privately.

I was afraid that people would notice that Filike was with

113

me; it was not permitted to take dogs down into a shelter. Why? Because when the shelling was going on, they could turn savage, bite, or infect. How numerous were the infections we feared then!

In the cellar were a pail of water and, right next to it, a mug with a handle; everyone dipped it into the water and drank from it. I thought the mug was dark-colored or dark gray. Then much later on, I once saw in daylight that it was originally white, the dirt on it gray.

Certain persons had food; others went up, when there was no firing going on, and obtained food from somewhere. We had nothing. I remember, I found a tiny package beside my head every morning. It must have been put there by János's aging, pudgy bachelor friend. A few cracklings; at another time one or two roundcakes, sometimes a piece of bread or sausage, or a bit of bacon in it. In any case, it was enough for Mami and me to get by on. I mean, we were hungry, but did not die of hunger.

Mami kept losing weight; she was no longer eating even what I found in the little package. I went to the doctor, János's acquaintance, and asked him what I should do. He advised me to give her liquids because otherwise she would die in the cellar. Fluids, yes, but what? We were limited to just one mug of water a day.

I went to the Russians and asked for a cup of milk. I knew what the price would be; I went to bed for a cup of milk.

Then I went to the parsonage, where we last lived. I wanted to fetch a mattress because the door was hard, and water had slowly soaked through it. The officer consented; if I would go to bed with him, I could take the mattress. (Which we had left there.) Filike was with me; it took place in the old potato cellar. There were still a few potatoes left; I lay on them, I did not move. Help yourself!

Meanwhile, the officer lit a match; first, he touched my eyes to see if they were open or not. They were open, he poked them; they hurt a little. But since I didn't move or flinch, he lit another match and looked to see if I was alive or dead. He shook his head.

He could not have derived much pleasure from me. But when I prepared to pack and take the mattress, he sent his orderly down, and he mounted me, too. Filike kept running around me, whining, whimpering, and licking my hand; my hands and legs were cold, the whining Filike's tongue was warm.

I made nothing of the fact that the officer had sent his orderly down. Today I am inclined to think that he was more democratic than Hungarian officers were. Or would a Hungarian officer also have sent down his orderly after himself?

This young soldier then helped me to hoist the mattress onto my back. We desperately needed the mattress because Mami was coughing and gurgling. I carried it happily. By now this no longer was a problem for me at all. We put the doubled-over mattress on my back and, bent in two, I moved on.

An air attack struck us on the way; I sat down in a ditch beside the road, the mattress over my head and back; I felt safe. A convoy of Soviet soldiers was traveling on the road; airplanes attacked it, nose-diving. To my surprise, this military convoy behaved just as the German convoy had previously: it slowed down. It is terrifying when the procession slows down and crawls along under attack, and it is terrifying when the planes above lose altitude and dive down with a ground-shaking roar and drone; but these solders leaned out, raised their machine guns skyward, and tried to shoot them down. When they spotted me under the mattress, they broke into cheers, shouted, threw kisses, laughed, clapped their hands: Bravo, bravo! (They knew this word; they used it frequently.)

I think what they enjoyed so immensely was something I didn't know, that the mattress would not protect me from anything on earth. Either a bullet or shrapnel would go through it, not to mention a blast or a bomb.

Much later, I was once again walking on the street with Filike. I wanted to die because I had reached the end of my tether, and the airplanes attacked again, the hurtling dive bombers. They swept along the road, the empty road; maybe they wanted to rip it up. I walked in the center of the road, I didn't want to seek cover. Let them hit me. "Oh Lord, let them hit me, let them hit me now," I begged. And still, when the plane was above me, roaring with its ear-splitting terror, the sound made me hunch my shoulders, and I crouched but moved ahead on my haunches. I didn't fall on my stomach, I didn't seek cover. I wanted to die, but I was unable to move standing upright. Filike, however, followed me without making a sound and faithfully. When I moved on my haunches, she gave me such a searching look and maintained the rhythm of my odd pace. (Filike, is there anyone on earth whose faithfulness is comparable to yours? And I abandoned you.)

Where was I going? To Mami. The doctor said she had to be removed from the cellar. She had a house, a lovely little peasant cottage with dark beams. She had rented it to an elderly couple. They took her in at my pleading; they took her in and also another old woman. As I learned later, they figured that safety was greater where there were old women, because the Russians liked the "little dolls" and "little mamas" and they greatly respected them. If it sometimes happened that they now and then took one of them away with the young ones, oh well, dear Lord, in the dark every cow is black.

One of the old women was wounded, and her wound became maggotty. She was very obese. "The old beast," said the master of the household.

I tried treating the wound, but I had nothing proper to use. I cleaned it with wine; I washed the bandage with snow, then left it out in the freezing cold to kill the bacteria. At the time, I did not know that maggots cleaned wounds. I fought them; meanwhile, I could not comprehend where the maggots could spring from into the body of a human being in winter.

Maggotty wounds – these belonged to the war, too. This is again something for which I cannot find an expression. The wriggling grubs appear in the human body, in the living, raw flesh – there where the wound ulcerates, secretes, suppurates; sometimes they tumble about; sometimes they pause, feeding for certain at such times. They are white, and of varying size – they teem.

In short, I placed Mami with the elderly couple for her safety. She lived well there, generally, and she was always urging, "Come, my child, come." At other times she warned, "Don't come, shooting is going on." But I went to her whether there was any danger or not.

While we were still living in the cellar, where people bickered and were impatient and edgy, we were often told how truly rare it was for a mother and daughter to love each other so much; we never raised our voices to each other. I corrected them. Mami was my mother-in-law, not my mother. They were amazed, they hardly wanted to believe me.

Mami was good, neat, simple, and reserved. We saw eye to eye in everything, much more so than I did with my own mother, or anyone else. I could never get along better with any man or woman than I could with Mami, despite the fact that we lived together in midst of dangerous situations and great adversity all the time. Maybe she was an angel. She embodied peacefulness, gentleness, and temperance. These hackneyed words express what she was like.

I loved her, and she loved me. Even when I began my search for János and begged that he not be put to death and not be taken away, she urged, "Don't go, stay here, don't go, you will run into trouble." And when they brought the news that János had been executed and I retorted it was not true, she looked at me, smiling, "You say it isn't? Are you sure it isn't? Let's not be afraid!"

The following episode took place while we were still living in the cellar. I wasn't present – I'd been taken away to dig trenches, I think (but more about what it meant to a woman to dig trenches in frozen ground later). On my return, I was greeted with the news that János had suddenly staggered into the cellar and shouted my name. It was then that the men were being herded out of the village, and he asked someone for a hat. He was still in his lounge jacket and slippers. In that terrible cold and snow. Hearing this, I thought my heart would break.

Her heart bursting, also the ground beneath,
And her little child falling into it.

Since that moment, I know the language of balladry contains psychological realism. Because this is what humans feel: the heart breaks, the ground splits asunder, and one plummets into the depths of darkness.

I was aware by then that János's manuscripts had been carried off. I had a piece of paper in my possession. During the night, I put his verses together line by line. I racked my memory until I found and wrote down every word, every line. Then I wrote in tiny letters in the margins, then sideways, backwards, and on the back of the paper. I filled the piece of paper with fourteen or twenty of his poems that I knew and that, though I had not learned them by heart, I was able to quote at the time. Then the Russians took away this sheet, too.

When we became infested by lice in the cellar, I undressed, so I could remove them from my undergarments. The woman behind me screamed. When I took off my slip, I had torn open the wound on my back. Horrified, she questioned me closely, "Didn't you notice you had a sore on your back? Didn't you realize you would tear it open?" Others ran over to look at the sore. (I got the sore because when the Russians raped me, they pushed my legs against my shoulders.) Later, the wound healed somehow; who could be concerned about it at that time?

Later we became scabby. The town clerk of Gyuró offered his felicitations to someone with these words, "Madam, what you have between your fingers is not a rash, it is scabies; I have it, too." I already knew so much about lice that I could tell which was female, which was male, which was pregnant, which was full, which was hungry. Sometime, I'll describe what lice are like. For now, briefly, there are hair lice, clothing lice, crab lice. Crab lice live in the hair of the armpits and in pubic hair, hair lice, as their name states, in the hair on the head. If you have all three, then it is futile to pluck them out, they bite you constantly. We were advised to smear ourselves with kerosene. The lice did not recoil from it at all, and the kerosene stung even more fiercely, and we became smelly, besides. Of course, there was no possibility of washing up.

At first we spoke about our mouths being smelly because we could not brush our teeth. Then, after a time, such a notion never occurred to us; we were not even aware of it, not even of the lack of washing up. With eighty of us in the cellar, there was not even enough water for us to drink, and, after a couple of days, our demand for water to wash up also ceased. On the other hand, it was horrible to bleed so profusely and not be able to put on clean panties. The blood froze in the trenches, it thawed at night; then it dried, and the panties pinched the thighs, and you always felt you smelled of blood. But then, everything around us smelled of blood.

A bomb exploded near us, the entire cellar shook. Silence followed. In the dead silence of eighty humans, a small child cried out. Then a woman's voice, pitched peculiarly high, began in a steady, monotonic rhythm, "Hail, Mary, full of Grace, the Lord is with thee, blessed art thou among women, and blessed is the fruit of your womb, Jesus. Holy Mary, Virgin Mother of God, pray for us sinners now and at the hour of our death. Amen." (Silence. Forty years later, that voice still rings in my ears. I must open a window.)

I thought I would go mad; I wanted to shout for her to stop, it was unbearable. But, I wonder, would it have been easier to endure the silence? Why did this prayer strike me as being so terrible? At the time I did not know it. This prayer is also the prayer of the dying. Since that time, I have become fond of it.

What is better in the face of a threat to life? For everyone to be silent, or for everyone to yell, for someone to pray, or for many to shout? I don't know. But fear is terrible if many are afraid, and fear is terrible if you are alone. Fear is somewhat more bearable if a Filike is with you and even somewhat more bearable if someone you love is beside you. How strange that I loved Filike but felt no fear for her. (As if she were invulnerable. As if she were one with me. And as if she never experienced any fear, she never whimpered, never barked. Sometimes she shivered, but dachshunds do that frequently.)

Once a Russian soldier came into the cellar. I was asleep. He woke me up; he bent over me and shook me. The same woman who had noticed the sore on my back told me that my face took on the terrorized look of a horse. My nostrils widened and quivered, the veins on my forehead swelled, and my pupils dilated queerly. This occurred at the first moment. Then followed my pleading, my begging in Rumanian. I implored the others in Hungarian, the kommandatura is nearby, go and tell them! ask for help! or send a child, you know the Russians will not hurt children. But no, not one of them moved. Eighty beings listened to my pleas and did nothing. I showed them I would cover the pistol's barrel, I would put my hand over it, so the soldier would not be able to shoot. They were afraid, they kept silent and tolerated my being raped right in front of them and the children. I wonder how they will square this with their consciences. And how will

I be able to if I do not help someone because I am afraid – and how many the times I will fail to help?

When there are screams on the street outside, I wake up from the deepest sleep. I run out to the balcony to investigate what is happening; I think I will throw something down, a vase, a potted plant. I have to do something because someone has called out for help, and I know people will not leave their apartments. When I called for help, no one budged. When I shouted for help out on the street... Yet people were there, looking out their windows. (Fear, not love, conquers all?)

No one took me in on the night I escaped from the parsonage. Much later, I needed help on a street in a small town in Hungary. I pleaded in vain for people just to let me into the cellar or to a chair in a vestibule or into the barn. No! No! During winter, it is not possible to spend the night without a roof over your head. In any case, by the time day breaks, you are exhausted, and if you sit down, you freeze to death. I am afraid when I am out on the street alone at night in a strange town. I might also fear I may be attacked; this does happen during a time of peace, in Budapest, too. But I am more afraid of being shut out.

Miklós once said they attack me because I am like a closed box to them, and they are curious about what is inside. I simply do not know. Anyway, the Russians attacked me many times. I learned I cannot fight a man; I am weaker, I cannot defend myself. I cannot hit him because he hits harder. I can not run away because he will run me down. There is nothing useful in the advice to kick the attacker's sexual organs, to kick him between the legs – as they now say, kick him in the balls! You can kick the first one, but in the next instant you are on the ground, and then most likely, you will never get up again because they will finish you off.

But as for why so many in the cellar were afraid, why they did not dare to help me? That they did not is understandable, but I still wonder about it on the rare occasions when it still comes to my mind.

The Russians took us to dig trenches occasionally, and it was excruciating, hacking the frozen ground with a pickaxe between continual bomb hits. But they gave us something to eat. At other times, we helped in the kitchen, which was a large, half-shot-up room. A soldier stacked the fire under the wash boiler, the cauldron pipe led through an empty window frame into the yard. The door was open – or was the door gone? We still felt some warmth, though. The cook's foot was missing; the stump was bandaged, he did the cooking like that. The Russians were incredibly brave; pain and fear had no meaning for them.

They prepared soup frequently; they boiled the water in a huge cauldron, tossed chunks of beef into it, then large amounts of cabbage and bay leaves, then potatoes and finally a handful of dumplings. I don't know what this soup was called; it had a very good flavor. Of course, it was no fun cooking for several hundred men.

We peeled potatoes in the cold, squatting on the ground until we thought our backs would break. We were given a dish of soup; I took mine to Mami. We were given the potato peels. We took some to those who were hungry, and we set some aside for spring planting. We stealthily peeled them rather thick, so that they would retain their buds. For by then, in February, it was obvious that the war would not be over by spring, that there would not be a potato crop.

One morning, the Russians gathered the women together again, and a young boy took it upon himself to save me from the round-up. He lay down beside me and put his arms around me; I covered my face, and somehow remained there. But an hour later they mustered the men. I said to the boy, "Now I will help you to stay here." I scattered straw, clothing, this and that over him; I rummaged about to hide him. There were not enough males around, so they took me away, too. I had two small roundcakes for that day. I gobbled them down and drank my ration of water on it, thinking that the Russians would give me something to eat. But the officer dressed the soldiers down for bringing women to perform such hard work, and I was chased back to the cellar. I had wolfed down the roundcakes! The others were amused by this, and so was I.

We were all extremely hungry when someone brought fresh bread to the fourth resting place on my left, to the woman who had called out the "Hail, Mary" so loudly. They cut into the loaf and started eating it. I became so agitated, I wanted some so badly, I broke into a sweat, and I considered going over to them, or sending a child, to offer my only

121

treasure, a small bottle of Vetol oil, in exchange for a small piece of bread.

I was holding on to a small bottle of Vetol oil, a German oil for wounds, at that, in the buttoned-down pocket of the checkered blouse I have mentioned. I guarded it like a treasure, though I had noticed that when it was applied, the wound filled with puss, instead of healing. But I did not have anything else, just a safety pin and a small piece of dried-up, moldy sausage, which I was saving until the very last, so that in case I or someone else should faint from hunger, something would be available. (I did save it from the war and reached liberated Budapest with it. And then... But what about *until* then?)

I did not dare go over to the woman to propose the exchange. I don't know how it happened, but to me it was like a miracle, like an embodiment of goodness, as if the firmament had opened up. She sent her child over to me with a small, fresh, real, soft, fragrant piece of her bread. I ate it very slowly, so that I could savor it at leisure. The pleasure of the bread, which we had been without for weeks by then, the pleasure of eating, the pleasure of goodness – this is what that piece of bread meant to me.

The Germans returned, then the Russians came again. I was always more afraid of the Germans. When they said there would be an execution, then you could be certain they would execute someone. The fear began with the Gestapo, and it was regressive. The persecution of the Jews intensified it.

With the Russians, you could never know anything, never figure out anything. It is amazing that something actually developed from this lack of organization. When they left, they never said good-bye; they simply vanished. When they returned, they greeted us with tremendous joy, took us into their laps, tossed us into the air, as if they were meeting their dearest relatives. They were warmhearted but unusually impulsive.

First, we learned to swear from them. *"Job tvoju"*[35] was the first real Russian phrase. Once a real misunderstanding arose. We wanted to say *"muzh jesty,"* that "I have a husband," meaning "don't harm me, it will bring me grief." *"Muzhna"* meant "you can"; they generally understood *"muzh jesty"* as "*muzhna*". According to them, when they took a woman away, she was desperately shouting "you can, you can." It could be translated approximately like that. It made no difference what they understood. It did not change anything.

A woman in the cellar is saying, "I went out and saw all was kaput." Someone asked her, "What did they do with every gate?" Laughter: "*kaput*" in Russian means something is over, ruined, or something like that.[36] In any case, we learned "*kaput*" and used it frequently. "Front jargon" developed quickly. The expression "*zabrálni*," "*to loot*," was the most natural, for it was close to *zabálni*, "to eat your fill like a pig." I don't know how we came to forget it today; after all, we continued to use the expression for twenty years.

The cellar did not give us any bright moments, any jolly times. Hunger, destitution, filth, lice, and sickness weighed us down; also, the constant fear and, naturally before and above all else, the outgoing and incoming firing, sometimes Russian, sometimes German.

We noticed, or thought we noticed, that three days of unbridled pillage followed every larger battle or reoccupation. Unbridled pillage and unbridled rape. After that, all this was forbidden, and generally, anyone who could be proved to have raped a woman would be shot.

I do not know how it came about, but I once found myself in a situation in which soldiers were standing in a row and I had to point out the one who had raped me. I remember it only faintly. On a cold winter morning, I am walking in front of the row; the soldiers are standing stiffly, straight, at attention. Two officers escort me on my left. I saw fear in the eyes of one of the soldiers. He had blue eyes and was quite a young boy. From this fear I knew he was the one. But what flashed in his eyes was so keen, so dreadful that I immediately felt: it is out of the question! There was no sense in having them kill this boy. Why, when the others would go free? And why only this one?

On another winter morning, however, they flogged me. I no longer know exactly why they did it. I don't even want to untangle it; somehow it has all become snarled (like so many other things). They stripped me to the waist, some soldiers stood around me, and one of them struck me in a regular rhythm. The lash was not a whip, but a pliable braided strap shaped like a snake, tapering off toward the end and terminating in a knob. Of course, it had a grip. When they hit someone hard, the skin tore open. (It did not hurt particularly, or it is possible that it did but that there was some sort of defiance within me or something else I have not spoken about before. I was able to take all that horror from beginning to end because the greater horror above everything else was that they had taken János away and the way they had done it. This completely occupied me, as did seeing the destruction of the village, and what was happening to women, children, and men; and I lived, of course, with the consciousness that this was going on throughout the entire country.)

Another time – I no longer know what happened – they injured me and then carried me to the Russian doctor in their arms. He bandaged me, petted me, and took me to the military dining hall for dinner. There was, it seems, something to eat that day. They served me chicken soup; then they cut off the end of a loaf of bread, removed the soft part, and filled it with the livers of all of the hens. Eight or ten livers to take with me. It was, of course, an unheard-of treasure. I ran to Mami's with it.

This is what the Russians were like. They hit me with one hand, petted me with the other. Sometimes they came to grips over me: one wanted to spare me, the other to rape me, one to beat me, the other to heal me. One to take something from me, the other to give me something.

They often showed up beaming, bearing this or that as a gift for us. Then it turned out they had stolen it from one of the neighbors. We often took our things over to the neighbors for safekeeping; they stole them from there and unsuspectingly presented them to us as gifts. But then, we were not exactly angels, either; we laid our hands on their belongings, and they did not get angry about it. In general, a kind of joint ownership existed during the war. Maybe it is humorous for me to use that expression, but it hits the nail right on the head. Only slowly did we catch on. When we all were going hungry, they shared their last bite with us.

By then we were eating rarely and little. Marianne's grandmother and Klári also wound up in the cellar. The old woman gave a Napoleon gold piece for some soup. She had the soup brought in secretly, and they ate it without sharing it with anyone. There was not enough for everyone, anyway. The fact that we had taken them in to save them and they ate what we had with us – well, that did not count. This did not distress me particularly, I just thought it was strange.

Marianne lent me a leather belt; my loose-fitting coat was warmer if I tied it at my waist. Then one time, two years later, they looked me up in Budapest and asked me to return the belt. I was greatly astonished by this. In addition, they asked for an Esterházy rug, claiming it belonged to them. Why was it theirs, or why was it ours?

In the beginning, the two hunting dogs were still with us at the parsonage. I don't know whether they were mates or from the same litter or cousins, but they were very fond of each other. They were big and strong; Filike, on the other hand, was tiny and fragile. I was on very friendly terms with the two dogs; they were with me most of the time, but I didn't take them into the cellar with me. One morning, while János was still with me, the Russians shot down one of them. The eyes of the other dog showed it was suffering greatly. It was suffering indescribably. It clung to me, but when I jumped out of the window and Filike followed me, it remained in the house.

Its name has been somewhere in the back of my mind for days, but even now I cannot say it; somehow I hear its sound, and the name just won't come to me. This dog spotted me from the gate of the parsonage as I was walking on the other side, and, running happily, it crossed the road, bounding toward me, its eyes beaming. A truck approached. I yelled out its name so it would stop, but it did not. It was hit in the middle. It raised its back slightly, looked in my direction, then jerked once or twice, and stretched out. I took Filike into my arms and covered her eyes, so she could not see it. Snow was falling. When I went back that way again, it was pulled a little to the side, so military vehicles would not flatten it into a pancake, and snow had already half covered it.

But I knew, felt it was better this way. What could I have done with such a big dog, an Esterházy hunting dog? I could not have taken it into the cellar with me. It was a miracle that the Russians had put up with Filike up to now; they gener-

125

ally shot dogs. The Germans liked dogs, the Russians liked children.

The inhabitants of the cellar suddenly discovered that Filike was with me. Scandal, uproar: there is enough trouble because of me, the Russians are searching the cellar because of me, the Russians are fleecing them, get rid of the dog!

I went to Mami's place and asked them to take Filike in. They accepted her very reluctantly. Filike would not eat, though she was given some milk and meat. (Such fare was a miracle by then; I don't know where they got hold of them.) But she did not eat a thing for two days. When I went over and she saw me, she ran to me and kept nipping my hands and ankles in her happiness. It hurt, but she kept nipping at me in her joy. Then she ate, but only if I stayed beside her, and meanwhile, she kept her eyes on me constantly.

Two days later I went over again. I encountered Filike in the yard and called her to me. She turned her head to the side to avoid looking at me and moved on. I cried and begged, but she did not want to acknowledge me. If I stood in front of her, she went around me, looking away indifferently beside me.

I parted company with Filike. She was safe, but I felt completely lonely. I never cried again during the war. After this, I was unable to cry for years. Those around me died one after the other, they came and went or were taken away. I gradually became indifferent toward them. But amid the dreariness of the days in the cellar, the filth, the lice, and the people quarreling and bemoaning the loss of their valuables, Filike was my last companion.

I covered myself with a black scarf and smudged my face with ashes and mud – this was how the women tried to protect themselves. One time, I had to jump over a ditch. I was wearing white Halina-cloth boots with black toes and heels. They were beautiful Hungarian boots. János had brought home the Halina cloth from the Russian front, and a boot-maker for officers made them for me in Kolozsvár. While jumping I neglected, for an instant, the stooped bearing of an old woman. The commanding officer of the kommandatura saw me from a window. Then he found me. I have no idea how he was able to do so. Soldiers dragged me to him, or rather, they escorted me as if I were going to an official interrogation. The kommandatura was situated next to the cellar.

He received me gently. I was served a good dinner. I waited for what was to follow. If I stay with him for the night, he said, he will give me half a pig. Good Lord! half a pig!

I went to bed with him without hesitation. Here there was cleanliness and order. Even something like a window with glass panes. Maybe the only one in the whole village. Touching me in bed, he said that some kind of discharge was draining from me – 'voda' (water). Maybe he even asked if I was sick. How would I know! After so many Russians who could know whether there was any syphilis or gonorrhea? "I don't know," I said. Somehow he relaxed. He was very gentle and pleasant; this affected me more painfully than being raped without any bargaining. Nevertheless, I tried to "behave." I wanted to leave early in the morning. I asked him to let me go. I was walking in the corridor. The woman cook, who was also the cook at the hospital, was coming toward me; she was cooking here now. She looked at me, the hospital's "little darling." I had gone to bed, even though they did not beat me, did not strike me; it showed in her eyes what she was thinking, "You are a whore."

Actually, I was a whore in the strictest sense of the word. A whore is someone who goes to bed for money or some other kind of benefit. A whore is someone who deliberately acquires something with her body.

Of course, this never entered my mind there. I did not think of anything. I did no thinking. Only some great bitterness abided within me. I felt it was unbearable, and not just this, but everything, the totality. What a gray morning! What is a gray morning? The nadir of human humiliation. I did not receive the half of a pig. I felt relieved.

Mankind turns savage and incomprehensible in war.

As early as autumn, János had shown me the lovely, large house his father had wanted to buy and in place of which he bought the smaller peasant house on the sidestreet. It was situated on a thoroughfare, on this side of the manor house; its stucco-decorated ceiling had taken a hit. A sofa had shot up to that ceiling and somehow remained stuck there. (I have often thought that if by chance they had purchased that house, maybe we would not be alive by now.) I once observed a Russian soldier, standing on a single board, fire zealously at the stucco, or what remained of it, breaking into pieces a house that had neither a front nor sides, just a back wall, all of the roof, and a ceiling with a sofa hanging from it. Much later, I learned from one of Miklós's novellas why in war soldiers shatter what remains standing.

As I have related elsewhere, the German soldiers did not overly respect the Esterházy manor house. They threw jars of jam against the frescoes, they kicked the beautiful antique furniture. I have already related how the Esterházys knocked out the bottoms of several hundred wine barrels and how people hauled away the wine in buckets, cursing the Esterházys. The Esterházys, however, warned everyone not to leave wine cellars full, and pour out all their wine. How did they know this had to be done? From history.

Then we, too, had to learn the lesson. Drunken Russians, drunken Germans were much wilder than the sober ones. In general, we were afraid when we encountered drunken soldiers.

Ah yes, the Hungarians feared for their wine. They all guarded their own cellars.

The Russians respected the manor house even less than the Germans had. They couldn't figure out how to heat the embossed and glazed earthenware stoves that stood on brass legs, or they didn't want to learn how from direct experience, although you could heat very effectively with these stoves, and they held the heat until the next day. Instead, they broke the windows, if by some chance they were still unbroken; then they boarded them up, ran the pipe of a small iron stove through an opening, and provided heat that way for the chambers of the manor house, as in a shack. The parquet floors were ruined; there was smoke, it pinched their eyes; they scattered straw on the floor and lay down. They smashed the majolica stoves into bits.

One of the hall-sized rooms at the manor house once served as a first aid station; I don't remember whether it was for male or female soldiers. Once I was taken there to work. Of course, shelling was going on, incoming and outgoing, as always. They brought in the wounded on stretchers, in their arms, on their backs, in whatever way they could. They laid them down on the straw that covered the entire hall. Stench, blood, brandy, mud, drenched clothing, sweat, the smell of foul breath were everywhere. The wounded did not cry or moan a lot. One or two women with rubber gloves reaching to their elbows bustled about among them. Why were they wearing those gloves? To protect their hands? Or the wounded from bacteria? I don't think so, because they were lying in the straw, in their fringed, torn clothing, in excrement, blood, filth, snot, mud. And the nurses were not in the habit of protecting their hands.

The nurses ordered me to help them. They sent me to a soldier whose fingers hung down, badly mangled. I asked them what I should do, in what language I don't know, maybe in Rumanian. But I may have known enough Russian by then. Save as much as you can, bandage it, they said, and cut off all the rest. "With what?" I asked. "With scissors," they replied. "Find some scissors and cut them off." I was horrified; this did not conform with my hygienic training. (Ultimately, what would be lost in this case? If we did not cut them off, gangrene would set in. But to lop off the fingers of a still conscious being with filthy scissors without any anesthesia? I could not do it.) Defying the probability that they would beat me up or shoot me, I turned around and walked out.

The intestines hanging out and so on and so on – I do not want to describe any of this. The female medical orderlies, like women preparing for a holiday in some kitchen, issued orders, shouted to each other, the male medical orderlies, and the wounded – their frame of mind was not at all solemn. It was as if they were enjoying the enormous commotion, and thought they could be the masters of the situation. I wasn't capable of this. I think they held me in contempt for it.

I saw a soldier whose foot was missing at the ankle, and sitting on a horse, he fought on with blood seeping through the bandage. (It is possible I saw this earlier.)

A soldier's left arm had caught a round of bullets. They produced a hatchet, sharpened it, and they kept giving him drinks, so that when he was unconscious from drunkenness, they could chop off his arm. In general, they got their wounded thoroughly soused; then they themselves had a go at it. This was the procedure also used in the Middle Ages.

The Stalin-organ?[37] When the Stalin-organ went off, the ground shook under our feet, black smoke suffocated us, and we fled in fright into the house. But we just heard it. What could those it hit have felt? And the Stalin-candle. A candle

129

descends slowly from the sky at night, it lights up the area with a bright light. The shelling can commence! When an air attack came, the Russian soldiers ran out of the houses, held their machine guns up, and fired at the planes, laughing all the while.

I went back to the parsonage one more time because of the Yugoslav priest, who still lay there sick and abandoned.

It was at the parsonage that Mami had cursed clergymen. When we were all still living there, the archdeacon, that hard, materialistic, avaricious man, stated that the house was the target of so much trouble because I, the "Protestant," was living there. The blue eyes of gentle, sweet Mami flashed, "You are not worth as much as this woman's little finger. If God is punishing this house, it is because of you clergymen. I am up to here with you. What counts is what you do and not what you say." From that time on, Mamika never again had anything to do with the clergy.

Others told me about this later. I listened dumbfounded. The archdeacon's judgment, who was raised in the religious freedom of Transylvania, was so incomprehensible to me that I felt no anger. I would have laughed in his face, if it had not hurt Mami's feelings so much.

I made arrangements with the nuns to take care of the priest. They accepted the responsibility. We managed somehow to put him on a door; I asked some soldiers to help us to carry him. They did. The priest's eyes filled with tears; he kissed my hand and said in German (I didn't know German, nor did he), "Gnädige Frau, Sie sind so gut. Sie müssen katholisieren." [38] I understood this. I found it quite humorous, but I didn't want to hurt his feelings. I said, fine, I will give it some thought. I did not know then that ten years later, I would be giving it some thought—and I would do it during the Rákosi era. [39] At the time, in the great bustle when everyone was rescuing their belongings, I abandoned the metal box in which I had hidden my jewelry and china. It remained under the bed on which the priest had lain. Just imagine, the Russians kicked it, and the china and the straw-like material in which it was packed fell out. They found it uninteresting and kicked it back under the bed. To my great amazement, while everyone lost their belongings, I found the box and took it home. Strange that I said, "took it home." I took Nyunyuka and the box from the parsonage to Auntie Anna's house. I shall relate how I got there.

I heard from someone that an interpreter named Benő Jakab could possibly find out something at the command post about our men who had been taken away: about János. I was told where his house was located. I went there. It was a small peasant house. I was aware that Russians lived in the front part of houses everywhere; so I knocked on the little window of the summer kitchen, the size of a cubby-hole, in the rear. An old woman peered through it and came out. She was Auntie Anna.

Auntie Anna is very difficult to describe. A peasant, her looks aging, a widow, black scarf, very humble, very deaf, slight, short. As I learned later, her husband had treated her very roughly, he thrashed her soundly. Anna went to do washing just because her life became easier for a couple of hours. She had a son, she loved him deeply. She had not heard a word about him for a long time; he was reported missing in action. Her daughter, Rózsika, was living with her, and it was her husband, Benő Jakab, who was the interpreter. He was from Upper Hungary and could speak to the Russians in "Ruthenian." (They had fled to this area from the bombardment of Budapest.)

By occupation Rózsika was, people said, a real whore. Then she married Benő, who made a lot of money as a sleeping-car guard. They built a nice house; Rózsika had a coat made of tiger fur and some jewelry. A long time later, they had a car accident, and Benő died at the scene. Rózsika was afraid of a storm, and Benő was driving too fast, so they would avoid it. She once looked me up in Budapest – I was Miklós's wife by then – and this was how we learned about their fate.

Rózsika had a "difficult" temperament, like her father; she treated Auntie Anna dreadfully. It was odd that she accepted me like a sister. She told me many times, "I love you like a sister." She never treated me badly.

Auntie Anna came out and contemplated my eyes for a long time. Benő is not at home, come in and sit down. I was afraid because she was full of lice and who knew what else. I sat cautiously, I did not take off my shawl. She urged, "Take off your shawl, it is hot."

It was a tiny summer kitchen, with a dirt floor, a stacked whitewashed stove, behind it a narrow bench-like bed with plaited bulrushes along the wall, to the side a bed, a small table, a wood table cobbled together under the window, and a chair. That was all the furniture. There was only a narrow space between the stove and the bed. In the very front, a door led from a lovely, cement-floored kitchen; opposite to it was a thin door made of boards, a tiny woodshed, a tool house.

Rózsika related to me later that when I knocked on the door, Auntie Anna said, "Mary knocked on the door, the Virgin Mary." She felt such purity and sadness emanating from the woman standing before the door that she had to be admitted. If she was not – she asserted to Rózsika – then she would be turning Mary away. I did not make anything of this; I came to know Auntie Anna as a perfectly clearheaded woman.

The next morning, the Russians again mustered the women and men in the cellar to dig ditches. Just then, Benő came with the soldiers; I did not know him, but he recognized me from Auntie Anna's account. There was a tobacco shop, completely demolished, at the assembly point; its door was missing, and inside were pieces of furniture thrown helter-skelter. "Hide under the table quickly, " Benő said, "I will come back for you." I crouched there for an hour or two; I froze to the bone; it was wintry cold. Then he came for me and said, "I will take you home." He took me home. To Auntie Anna, to the tiny, clean summer kitchen.

Benő left. Auntie Anna heated some water and brought in a washtub. She and Rózsika seated me in it and gave me a bath. They washed my undergarments, my panties (they were encrusted with blood). While those were drying, Rózsika gave me another pair to wear. This was a very great thing for her to do under the circumstances.

From that moment on, this was my home. They gave me something to eat. Auntie Anna slept on the floor, literally the dirt floor; doubtless, there was a draft between the two doors. Rózsika and Benő slept on the narrow straw mattress on the bed, and I on the bench-like bed.

The days passed peacefully in the beginning. No one harmed me. I do not know whether it was then or later that Péter appeared on the scene.

Péter was nineteen, a Soviet soldier. He took a fancy to me. The upshot was that he did not want to rape me. For a defense, I began by telling him I had a problem with my heart. "No," he said, putting his hand on my dress, on my thigh, "I don't want this." Then putting his hand on my heart, "This is what I want!"

He explained that in Russia there are streets with sidewalks, canals where the water drains, and there is never any mud. You can turn a small wheel, and pure, delicious water flows from the faucet. You can buy as many cabbages and potatoes as you wish. And you can buy bread every day.

He related all this as if Russia were a fairyland, so I would be seized by the desire to go with him. He wanted me to become his wife. In the morning he would go out into the yard and sing full-throatedly, *"Viorita moya zhenka budiet."* [40] I caused a minor mishap on one occasion. I was seated, and Péter laid his head in my lap. Wanting to resist, I raised it, Péter turned his head to the side, and my finger poked him in the eye.

The other soldiers rushed in because I wanted to poke out the eye of a Soviet soldier. Péter yelled, *"Viorita ne hotyila!"* [41] Then Rózsika came, then Auntie Anna followed. Auntie Anna wept and pleaded. Benő came and said it was not intentional. Wrangling. Finally, they let me go because of Péter's fury.

German planes showered leaflets down from the sky. Russian soldiers dashed in, to show them to me, for me to read and tell them what they said. I told them I did not know any German. They were terribly insistent. I still remember that the large-lettered heading went something like this, "Soviet forces retreated 50 kilometers at Lovasberény." I really did not know German, but *"50 kilometers zürück,"* and *"sowietische truppen"* – this was possible to understand. I reported it to them. They looked at me, folded up the leaflet and left, and in the evening of that day, they took me away under the suspicion of being a spy.

I do not understand even today why I did not want to die right then, why I didn't want them to execute me. But I felt it was insane. Should I die because of this? When they stood me before the summary court, I tried to explain with the help of an interpreter that there are Gothic, Cyrillic, and Latin letters. The leaflet was in Latin letters and Arabic numerals, which were also commonly used, and so I was able to read them. We Hungarians also used the word *"zürück,"* we have taken it into our language. Lovasberény was a Hungarian place name. It was even simpler to understand they were Soviet troops. They listened to all this attentively to the end, and obviously tried to evaluate it. They asked several times what a Latin letter was. I still remember the words *"bukva latina."* The interpreter did not know anything about it and kept shrugging his shoulders. I told him to ask anyone who had finished their schooling as to what it meant. They asked me three times whether we write with Latin letters and why we do. I explained that everyone in western civilization uses Latin letters. They greeted this with disbelief. (At the time Benő had been taken to another village to do some interpreting.) It was apparent that they thought the entire world used Cyrillic letters. Why were they unable to read our writing? They presumed it was all in German and based on some kind of secret agreement.

Night came. I waited for them to come to a decision. They were searching for a village teacher. Whether they would execute me or not depended on the courage, cowardice, or education of this individual.

They received the information that Latin letters actually exist. That "km" equals "km." We use the *'zürück'* word. In a jiffy, without further ado, "You may go!" They released me. This was the way they did it. Carrying out an execution was no special ceremony, either.

Sergei. I no longer know what happened when the three soldiers broke in – they wanted to take me away again. Sergei did not actually harm me; I only remember that he stood there and shouted when Rózsika started off to the command post for help because the soldiers were again raping women. At this, his companions fled, only he stayed behind. The patrol arrived. They gave him a good hiding and hauled him away. He returned the next day with two or three of his companions and shouted that he had been slapped because of me. In Russia, he said, equality exists between men and women. He stood me in the middle of the room to give me back what he had received. I thought he would slap me in the face so hard that my head would fly off and my teeth shatter. I got ready for it. I clamped my eyes shut; I stood with my feet set apart a little so I would not fall down. I waited for Sergei to hit me in the face. A monstrous crack! He had clapped his hands together, and he kissed me. Of course, the house rang with laughter.

Actually, this episode remains among my pleasant memories. This was the way they played pranks.

But Sergei was really badly injured; he was pale and furious when he was given the hiding.

Boxing each other's ears or fighting broke out among them with incredible suddenness; a storm of words followed, then died down; it became quiet as if nothing had happened.

The soldiers got hold of some flour and lard; it was possible to make some pancakes with them. We mixed flour and water and fried it in lard. No sugar, salt, there was nothing. But pleasure, yes. They stood in line, and Rózsika and I cooked and cooked pancakes constantly from morning until noon. We became worn out and very bored, and they kept clamoring; as customary with soldiers standing in line, they kept pushing, urging, demanding. Infuriated, Rózsika took the plate on which we put the pancakes, threw it to the ground, and shouted at them. She swore in Russian and adorned it with Hungarian.

The outcome: they calmed Rózsika down, picked up the remains of the plate, brought us another one, and quietly, not uttering a word, they continued standing in line. The soldier at the head of the line would always hold the plate, we would turn the pan over on it; he would bolt down the hot pancake and pass the plate on to the next one in line.

One night they drank a lot, caroused and shouted. But they left us alone. In the morning they told us to clean their room. Auntie Anna started off immediately. No, they objected. She was old, I should go. I went into the square room on the streetside for the first time. On the dirt-covered floor were cigarette butts, vomit, trampled scraps of food. Beside the wall were two gasoline cans, machine guns here and there (more like a gun with a short handle); and they sat, according to their custom, in their quilted, furred overcoats and watched me as I swept and then scrubbed the floor. They made fun of me and teased me because my white young woman's hand had to do some work. It was not easy. The vomit stank, and they did not move out of the way. I crawled under the chairs and washed around their feet. They guffawed. One of them put his boot on my hand; I felt that he wasn't really stepping on it, that he simply wanted to frighten me, but the damaged heel plate tore open the back of my hand. It was not a deep wound, but since I bleed easily, the blood flowed. Out of deviltry, I continued to wash the floor unconcernedly. A terrible storm erupted. Shouting. They swore at the soldier who had stepped on my hand, and, scurrying, they took me to the Russian doctor. He was also angry with them, and they showered me with gifts. (A spoon, a knife, two half loaves of bread, and a brightly colored summer dress.) Rózsika and I were greatly amused. This was the way we lived.

There were times when we had only plain camomile tea to drink without sugar, and, at noon, only watery grits boiled in salt water to eat. The Russians did not much care, either, whether they ate or not.

New units arrived while Benő was away, and I was harassed a lot, which I was finding very hard to bear. I moved to the neighbor's place; a family with five children was living there in a woodshed. They were being left alone because the man's broken leg was in a cast, and, besides, the Russians felt a respect for a family with five children. The seven of them barely had room in the woodshed. In it was stacked a cord of wood, on which Uncle Mihály (whose leg was broken) spread some straw, and I slept on it, covered with a rug. It was a good high resting place. But no matter what we did, I could always feel the logs. This would not have been a problem, because it is not important in a war for you to lie comfortably. But when things were quiet, red bugs would crawl out of the stack of logs, and since my body was warm, they would run around on me, beside the lice. When bombardment started, the bugs would hide. I could not sleep either from the firing going on or from the bugs holding dances on me. They were as immune to the kerosene we smeared on ourselves as the lice.

I eventually returned to the Jakabs.

I don't know what happened, what made me so dead tired. Somehow or other, I was no longer afraid of the soldiers, but I shuddered at the thought of having to wake up to a round fired into the lock and then having them enter; I shuddered at the thought that they could break the door in on me at anytime. Plus these – the perpetual removal by force, the fatigue, the filth, the illness inside me, the fevers. I just did not know how much more I could take. (There was no place to escape, we were right in the middle of the front, the very worst place in Hungary. The war surged back and forth between Bicske and Lovasberény for three months.)

Maybe the last straw came when a young woman eight months pregnant ran into a barn during a battle; a shell fragment struck her abdomen. First her intestines, then her baby spilled out, and the baby wriggled there on the ground. The mother shrieked and watched it before she died.

This was intolerable. There is no God. It is not possible that God would allow this to happen.

Auntie Anna, she was my sole source of comfort, purity, and goodness in life. (The firing line had separated me from Mamika.) Had the village changed hands or not? One could never be sure of anything.

Then once, when I could no longer go on, I looked at the concrete ring of the well, to bash my head to pieces against it. Another time I searched for a big rock to hit my head with and spatter my skull. There was no train I could throw myself in front of. Only the manor house had upper storeys, and it was full of Russians. Maybe I should have searched for a rope.

I want to recount a dream that haunts me in several variations since that time.

I am fleeing, the Russians are running after me. My legs seem made of lead, I have difficulty running, but I have to keep accelerating because they will catch up with me. A leafy, large tree. I clamber up, I fall back. They are already in my tracks; I can see their faces, their glances. Somehow I climb back up the tree. I keep climbing, I do not fall back, but they are also up on the tree behind me. I crawl out on a branch ever higher, rather ever closer to its tip. I fall and hit the ground. I race along. I reach a wall. I climb up the wall. I climb up the wall between the slots of the bricks to reach its top. My nails tear as the Russians jerk me back. I am running again, into a house. I flee back and forth inside the house. I go across attics, cellars, through doors, windows. They catch up with me. I run into a lavatory, I lock the door behind me. I know

137

they will break it in, but I have a second or two until then. I stand on top of the toilet, I reach into the tank, I know it contains a weight. I want to take it out and hit my head with it and shatter my skull. But by then they break the door in. The weight is in my hand. A Russian comes toward me, I want to hit him in the head. At that moment I wake up, sweating; I feel my heart throbbing in the corners of my eyes, I am suffocating, gasping for breath.

I had this dream for many, many years. It is beginning to fade now. But I am still wandering about in houses and fleeing, and the Russians are still opening doors on me and crawling through windows. I am now realizing, as I write this, that I shall always be apprehensive when a door stands ajar – who will come through it and pounce on me and take me away or deck me, hit me? But I do not like tightly locked doors, either. What an illusion they are (I learned from the Russians, how to open any door with a crowbar), I cannot escape quickly enough if the door is locked.

I poured some gasoline into a glass, and I said to Auntie Anna that if the Russians broke in on us again, I would throw the glass into the stove. A small fire burned in the stove day and night, so we would not freeze.

"Auntie Anna," I said, "when they break in the door, stand behind it. While it is exploding, the door will ward off the flames, and then you will jump out and run into the yard and quickly lie down in the snow. Be careful, cover your face."

Auntie Anna, who was so good and religious, a believer, looked at me and said calmly, "I will not stand behind the door."

I wonder whether the Russians sensed something in me. I don't know; they left me alone. Or maybe tranquility prevailed for a couple of days by accident. For otherwise, there was no tranquility. Incoming, outgoing firing, casualties, mud, trenches, lice, hunger.

Then the Russians evacuated the village, as I learned later. But we had no sign of it at the time. Had we, maybe I wouldn't have left with the Jakabs, because I did have to give thought to Mami. Usually, the Russians evacuated a village by entering houses with the order for all to leave in ten minutes. Then everyone tied everything they could into a bundle; those who had a wheelbarrow or something loaded their things on it, took hold of the children, and, being spurred on, moved quickly. Mami and the old women could not go on foot and remained in the house. Had I been there, maybe I would have tried to carry her away in a wheelbarrow.

Benő, Rózsika and I headed for Budapest, because I knew my mother and the family had fled to my great uncle Gábor's home on Wekerle Street.

We started out with a borrowed horse – it could barely walk – a wagon, and a little slip of Russian paper with Cyrillic letters on it, which Benő could read. It was very hard for me to say good-bye to Auntie Anna. In keeping with her wish, she remained in the house with the Russians. They never harmed her; they liked her because she was old, and they felt her gentleness and kindness.

She has died since then. If there is some kind of heaven, then Auntie Anna is there. (My friend Judit told me she didn't believe in God. Then all is fine with you, I said, because for you there is nothing after death. There is no accountability, no purgatory, no further suffering. There is nothing more than nothingness. "There is nothing," she said. Only scepticism and the possibility that maybe there is a God?)

We kept moving on and on. We pushed and pulled the wagon, the horse. Firing went on here and there; then came the abandoned ruins, the dead, but really not very many of the latter. We arrived in Budapest. It was in ruins, but we were surprised that, generally speaking, so many buildings were still standing; we thought everything had been pulverized.

We were stopped several times, but Benő produced the slip of paper, and we were allowed to continue. We reached the place where the Margit Bridge had once been. Many fabulous stories were circulating about the destruction of this bridge; my sister Irene's account belongs among them. She was just wanted to cross the bridge by streetcar. There was a long delay, she got off to pee. She did not make it back to the streetcar before it started up. So from the river bank she saw the bridge blow up, half of the middle streetcar remained hanging in the air, its other half plunged into the Danube. It was a bright morning.

When we reached the spot, the Russians were just in the

process of constructing an emergency bridge. I found the scene interesting. Two steep semicircles, one from Pest to Margit Island, right to its tip, the other from Margit Island to Buda. Everything was made of wood and piled up, the way buckets and boards were in Transylvania; they joined them together arched very steeply. The Russians were painting the bridge at the time. They did not want to let us across with the wagon, "Stop and paint the bridge!" I seem to remember, they were painting it red, but I won't swear to it. I grabbed a brush and painted.

March had arrived, but it was still cold. We had walked all day and had not had anything to eat. I wanted to reach my mother and family by nightfall. No one was permitted to be out on the street at night. (The curfew was in force.) I knew Russian fairly well by then; I said I was sick. I put the brush down and started to walk away. The Russians shouted that they would beat me up. But I talked back to them in Russian and just kept on going. They were dumbfounded and let me go on.

In the meantime, the Jakabs had somehow ridden away in the wagon. I had given them our address. If my mother and family are alive... But what if they are not? I don't know what I would have done. The oil for wounds and the small piece of sausage were in my pocket. Well, I started for Wekerle Street. I looked at the buildings, at those blown to bits, at those that survived. By this time there no longer were dead horses and corpses on the streets. After Csákvár, Budapest seemed peaceful and orderly.

I found 16 Sándor Wekerle Street. The back part of the building had burned down. Everything was black, sooty, cindery; I could see right through all the apartments. I stood and took it all in.

The building right next to Uncle Gábor's had fallen down, collapsed. Auntie Grünberg, whom I liked very much, lived there. (She had a two-room apartment with a kitchen. The two rooms had crashed down, but the tiny kitchen remained. She withdrew into it for sixteen years, hoping she would receive an apartment from the state. She fell ill, and the state paid her sixteen thousand forints in compensation, and she moved to the provinces on that.)

I went up the stairs slowly. The door had a bell, the old

bell. It seemed incredible to me. I rang. I no longer remember the way we met or what we said. There were many strangers in the apartment. My family had taken in the residents of the burned-out section.

There were no panes in the windows; their frames were pasted over with paper, instead. But I remember I was astonished and surprised to see the table spread with a white tablecloth. We had dinner, a real dinner.

We sat down and ate. I was full of lice and filthy; I had only washed my hands; nothing else entered my mind in the commotion present in the apartment.

Naturally, my mother wept and was happy and hugged me. I looked at her and was happy for her. I was happy they all were alive, though not very much so.

I myself wasn't very happy about anything and didn't much believe in anything. I was already carrying the sickness that would prevent me from ever giving birth to children, and I didn't know whether I had syphilis or not. I suspected that I could infect someone badly, and I did not want to infect anyone.

We were seated at the table; I did not even take out the little piece of sausage I had kept hidden to this point. It seemed ridiculous on this occasion. We were having tongue in tomato sauce. I looked at it, marveling; I ate it silently.

They told me the Russians had raped women. "Where you were, too?" asked my mother "Yes," I replied, "where I was, too." "But they didn't take you away, did they?" she asked. "Yes, everyone," I replied, and I kept on eating. My mother gave me a little look and said in amazement, "But why did you let them?" "Because they hit me," I replied, and I kept on eating. I did not consider the entire matter to be either important or interesting.

Someone asked airily and drolly, "Many times?" "I lost count," I said, and I kept on eating. "Just think, we had lice in the cellar," my mother said. "We did, too," I said. "But surely you didn't get infested." "I did indeed!" "With head lice?" my mother asked. "Every kind," I said, and I kept on eating. Then we talked about other things.

My mother called me aside after dinner and said, "My dear girl, don't tell such nasty stories, people might believe them!"

I looked at her. "Mother, it is the truth." She began crying and put her arms around me. Then I said, "Mother, I said they took everyone away, they raped every woman! You said they took away women here, too."

"Yes, but only those who were whores. You are not one," my mother said. Then she threw herself on me and begged, "My dear, tell me it is not true!" "All right," I said, "it is not true. They took me away just to nurse the sick."

We also met with my elder brother, Egon. I no longer remember those whirling days, either.

I recall more clearly my visiting the place where Egon was living with Márta and their showing me – we laughed about this, they were such precious moments – that they lived on the fourth floor and the third floor was missing below them. (Márta, Egon's lover, who had already popped up in our lives in Kolozsvár, was a physician and the same age as my mother. So my brother was in love with a woman the same age as my mother.)

They also told me that when the bomb hit the building, they were all in the apartment, and water was standing in many bottles and buckets because they could get water only now and then. Everyone hit the floor; all the bottles broke and water ran in streams. Márta's mother was wounded under the eye. Márta rushed over to take care of it and bandage it. Her other daughter and her grandchildren were not injured.

Egon went out, looked down at the gallery leading to the apartments, and saw that there was no apartment below them. He tiptoed back and said, "Don't anyone move! They shot out the apartment below us, we will stay here in the air!"

This was their good fortune. Namely, the columns of reinforced concrete held up the storey. The Russians did not dare go up, they left them alone. Egon had already had to flee previously because he was a military deserter.

Before they were to blow the building up, the Russians walled him and Márta up in the lavatory. They lived there for days or weeks. Water and food were lowered to them on a rope by way of the airshaft.

I told Márta what had happened to me and that I should go to a doctor because I felt I had an infection, most likely syphilis. She took me to a doctor acquaintance of hers. I had to wait a couple of days for the test results.

I remember that when I returned for the report, the doctor received me very gently and considerately. He asked me to take a seat. I knew from this that I was in for some bad news. This was the way they used to inform you.

Then he said, "Madam, unfortunately, the finding is positive." "Syphilis?" I asked, looking at him. "No, gonorrhea." Relieved and laughing, I stood up, "Just gonorrhea?" The doctor looked at me, astounded. He didn't know I was already intimately familiar with gonorrhea, nor was he aware of what I had gone through.

He asked me in astonishment, "This is 'just' to you?" He was right – "just" was an exceedingly hasty word, because it was not possible to get any medicine for it. According to my estimate, one-fourth of the country had gonorrhea, counting the troops stationed in it. There was absolutely no way of getting hold of medicines; quite simply, they did not exist. (Antibiotics were discovered only later, after the war; they reached Hungary much later.)

On the other hand, it is not advisable, as it turned out, to walk around with gonorrhea for a long time, as that also became evident. Of course, I had my suspicions.

How difficult it was to get hold of anything in those days and how people cheated! Egon, I remember, bought some Russian tea. The clerk weighed out the tea. He paid the bill. When they used it, they found a hooked nail in the bottom of the box.

But people did behave honorably, too. For instance, Uncle Gábor and his family took in other residents whose apartments had burned down and shared everything with them. At the time, no decent person ate – though hunger existed – without sharing food with others who were hungry.

Irénke had gone farther west on a German ambulance train. She was afraid of the Russians. Since she had a fear of the sick – she fainted at the sight of blood – she specified that she would do only office work. Then, because of typhus, she wound up in quarantine, where the nurses were also dying. She was often alone with the dying; she had to do everything for them. A young officer was unable to see because of a wound; he was blind. She was pushing him to a treatment in a wheelbarrow. Tihamér, while blind, fell in love with her. When he recovered, he was able to see again; he proposed to her; then, after they returned, he married her in Hungary. She became a splendid, courageous woman.

I learned this from her, "Your hand and foot will not hurt when amputated radically." (She nursed soldiers who were left only with their torsos; they kept them in clothes baskets.) I did not know all this about her at the time, only that she had left with the hospital. Pista Kovács also went to the west, or was he taken into the army?

No news about János and the others. How could it have possibly reached us? It seemed as if the entire country lay in ruins and some sort of migration had begun. Everyone was going somewhere with wheelbarrows, backpacks, half-wrecked bicycles, sleds, tottering wagons which people pulled with their hands or by harnessing themselves to them – they crawled along here and there. From Buda to Pest, from Pest to Buda. Probably the reason was that each one was seeking refuge, safety somewhere else because they were Jews, deserters, partisans, escapees, or because they simply feared bombardments and families were nestling closer together. Houses were collapsing and being gutted by fire – they had to move on, and now everyone was searching for a place.

The migration was hampered by the fact that the bridges had been blown up and had crashed into the Danube. Only one bridge remained half-passable. Somehow the Ferenc József Bridge had been patched up; there the lines of people, like ants, swarmed together, piling up terribly and tensely. (The Russians kept the small wooden bridge at Margit Island under guard, apparently for the delivery of supplies and for the guarantee of other things.) Of course, the capital also had more intact districts and quieter places. I saw these migrations at crossing-places. I myself had started from Sándor Wekerle Street for Castle Hill in order to locate the papal nuncio, Cardinal Rotta, and ask for his help in case he knew something about what happened to our men.

I made it across the bridge with great difficulty. A dead man lay at the Buda abutment, half onto the sidewalk – maybe people had pulled him away from the road. I had never seen anything like this before, a horrible vision with its own grotesqueness; his face completely flattened, he lay with open eyes, his expression fixed, his knees pulled a little toward his stomach. What accident had overtaken him? Who had left him there? Or was he completely alone, and who would remove and bury him? Police, stretcher bearers, and soldiers didn't exist and still weren't around. Then the Russians began to organize this service, too. Or had the city begun to recover itself so quickly?

I reached Castle Hill. The palace and the sections connected with it were in ruins, and, of course, many other buildings as well. The more deeply lying basin of the Vérmező was filled up with rubble from the ruins. The place where a park now blossoms was then a flat, deep basin overgrown with grass, the Blood Meadow; that was where the government executed the Jacobins;[42] we used to cross it on little paths. According to architect Pál Granasztói, the picture of the city was more interesting and individualistic then; now mothers stroll with their children and the elderly sun themselves there; sometimes young people sit half-naked on the grass. It was here, in 1959, that a man assaulted me among the flowering bushes in the softly sprinkling rain on a night in May.

I cut across on the path and climbed up among the ruins somehow. The nunciature was mostly undamaged. Someone in the building informed me that the nuncio was with the Mary Ward nuns on Veres Pálné Street.

I found him there. He knew nothing about the nunciature's representatives who had been taken away, but he complained bitterly and at length that he had to leave the country within three days; he was being sent back to Rome and altogether only two passenger cars were placed at his disposal; so he did not know whether he could take enough communion wine for the journey, and the cars were bumpy and tiring.

When I recounted to him what had happened, he told me, "We are all in God's hands, trust him, my daughter; I shall pray for them," and with that, he extended his hand for me to kiss his ring. Dismayed, I looked at him, and I began to feel nauseated. What does this man know about others? What does he know about the war? I already knew this much about Catholicism, that the amount of communion wine needed for a week fits into one bottle. (If he doesn't take too many swigs.)

I took the hand extended for the kiss and shook it, "I will

145

pray, Father, that the car will not jolt you too much and that you will have enough wine for your journey."

Today I laugh at myself, but at the time I was still a Protestant and young; I was pleading for János, and I had run into a rock of piety.

I headed toward home, toward my mother's apartment. I looked at the ruined buildings, the sky, the streets. I was searching for my place in it all. Whither? Where?

I was lying in a fever in Uncle Gábor's place, where László Cselkó and his wife had come for a visit. She had been János's sweetheart, his first love, when she was a girl. Later, I became very good friends with them, but then I was seeing them for the first time. They had received a letter from János; he had given them my great uncle's address, and they had come to turn the letter over to us. A few words were concerned with me, "My mother and my wife disappeared in the commotion of the war at Csákvár. I am not very likely to see them again." He wrote that he was a diplomatic prisoner of war. "I am well, I am treated well," and so on and so on. He did not write much about himself; I no longer remember the details. Only who he was with. At the time I skipped over this, they were foreign names. Later on, these names would become important. And, "Please inform my wife's mother or her relatives that they will not see their girl again during their life." That was all.

The letter began with lengthy chatter addressed to the woman, and what he wrote to her concluded very nicely and warmly. When I read the letter, a great weakness engulfed me; I thought I was going to faint. On the one hand, I rejoiced immensely at the fact that he was alive and well; but on the other, that cold sentence, "Please inform my wife's mother or her relatives that they will not see their girl again during their life" stabbed me to the quick. Was that all I meant to him?

We met with the couple one more time before we were to return to Kolozsvár. The woman told me I should not count on János. She saw him, met him during our honeymoon. When he told me that he was going to visit a friend in the hospital, he went to her and took her some flowers. She also told me that during those days, she also saw him at a nightclub. He

146

was sitting with a professional whore. It was probably then that he caught the gonorrhea.

Why did she tell me this? Because now that she had come to know me at age nineteen, and only recently coming out of the war, and having heard that I would like to go after János, that I wanted to find him, she felt sorry for me?

I loved János profoundly; I felt relieved, I rejoiced that he was alive. But what I had learned just now was so bitter that it made life unbearably difficult for me. Difficult? Farcical. No word can convey what it meant to me.

I thought the war was over. I thought easier times lay ahead. I was mistaken.

(Horsemen are passing by the front of our apartment; I see them in the mirror; looking up from the sheet of paper, I see them as they ride by on the street. They are foreigners, I gather; the tip of the island is an ideal area for riding horses.

How numerous were the horses in the war, these comrades-in-arms, and how very many of the dead horses we ate!)

PEACE

Somehow we dragged ourselves to our feet and started off to Kolozsvár. The day warmed up slowly; I remember we settled down on a flat, open, sideless carriage at the West Railroad Station, my mother, Márta, Egon, and I.

Night came and we were very cold. We stood on the tracks, freezing.

Next to us was a Russian military train; a soldier was guarding bales of compressed hay. Since I knew Russian, I called over to him and asked him to give us some. He stood up without saying a word, picked up a bale, and wanted to hurl it over. I held out my arms to catch it, he waved for me to stand to the side. He threw it. I now know that one of these bales of compressed hay weighs about a hundred or two hundred pounds. I must have looked silly wanting to catch it. As he threw it over, the powerful and easy movement was graceful. Bang, it fell among us. We made a huge stack with it and crawled into it. This way we were able to make it through the night easily.

The journey took about five days. One time, we found ourselves in a closed cattle car; we were waking up just as day was breaking. The train was at a standstill. There were about ten of us in one half of the car, another ten to fifteen in the other half. Everyone was packing up when the car started up. Bump, it started up with a jerk; we all fell headlong in one direction. We struggled to our feet, happy to be underway. Then, bump, a collision at that moment, and we all fell over, this time to the far side. Egon sat up and said it would be better for us just to stay put.

Switching was going on. When the switching engine bumped our car, we fell for the first time; when we struck the other car, we fell for the second time. We departed five or six hours later.

We were always happy while the train was moving. We were quite exhausted by the time we reached Várad. I was also running a fever.

I had secured a book on graphology in Budapest, the "Haynal and Balázs"; I read it and studied graphology during the journey. I had decided that I would earn money with this until I could obtain some kind of employment, because no matter how sick I was, how feverish, I would be able to carry on this line of work. And I did for a time. (I later came to know both of the authors personally; indeed, Dr. Haynal became my training analyst.)

We arrived in Várad. My mother had already become very fatigued by then, or at least that was what I told the Russians in the office there, and asked them to permit us to board a passenger train that was taking soldiers across Rumania. They gave me a document and allowed us to go aboard. I made good use of my knowledge of Russian.

It was already a regular passenger train. We stood in the passageway, of course. Beside me was a Russian soldier's bride with silk stockings on her legs. The package I was holding in my hand grazed her and she cautioned me in Rumanian, *"Dudue, vai ciorapi, aveti grija,"* which means, approximately, "Oh missy, look out for my stockings, they will get a run!" It was one of my biggest surprises, after all that had happened, that someone could be concerned about her stockings, but, at the same time, it was obvious that such a world as this did exist. I just hadn't thought that this world was close and would exist again and that I would be living in it once again. To me, it was, meanwhile, the world that had hied to the past, one that was gone, one that had vanished, and I couldn't possibly comprehend that stockings could also be a problem for anyone. I had many more problems of the hour, more immediate problems to contend with. I wasn't able yet to leave the atmosphere of death, famine, and filth.

Arriving in Kolozsvár, we got off the train, and since we were not aware that hansoms and taxis were already operating in the city, my mother hired a wagon. It was the kind of wagon used to transport logs, huge logs in Rumania; it had an axle with two wheels in front and an axle with two wheels in back and it was pulled by oxen. We got up on the pieces of timber and loaded our bundles on top, and hanging our legs, we headed for Unió Street, hoping that my father was still alive, that something still remained of the office and the building next to it. People looked at us in astonishment. In Kolozsvár, we encountered peace, quietness, tranquility, and well-dressed people; there was no trace of the war at all. And, most astounding after a starving Budapest, ham, sugar, rice, and flour were on display in the shop windows – peacetime shop windows. A picture still persists in the mind's eye: an enormous smoked ham rises from a mound of rice, rings of sausage arranged below. Wonder-struck, I gazed at it. At first I thought I was seeing a painting or a poster. We arrived in front of the apartment building. Egon ran up into the apartment.

My father came down, and the daughter of his lover at the time, Éva. Now, what was the name of this woman, her mother? Yes, it was Mac. She later committed suicide by cutting her wrists. Well, Éva kissed me, and my father did, too. His mustache gave off the same scent of cologne that Éva wore. And Éva's mother, too. For an instant a shiver ran down my spine. Was my father having relations with the both of them?

We quickly learned that my father still had his office and the front part of the apartment. His other lover lived in the back part, his former office girl, Bici, Éva's half-sister. Was my father having relations with every woman in this family? One time he said, yes, they had "come across each other." But I don't know anything definite about Éva; I never asked him about her.

So my father had remained there. When he parted from us at the railroad station, he went into a snack bar to have something to eat. Since the bridge had not been blown up – the word that reached us was untrue – he calmly strolled to his office and remained there in tranquility. Kolozsvár was under fire for only one day, and then, too, the railroad station was targeted again to prevent anyone from escaping.

Before the war, my family lived on Bercsényi Street in a four-room apartment, in a family apartment building with a garden, opposite my own apartment. My father had an office on Unió Street, consisting of a room, a vestibule, and a small, nicely furnished office; it was located in an old ground-floor apartment of a vaulted building. During the war, my father acquired lawyer Fischer's office, two buildings away, which took up all the rooms on the second floor. A separate stairway led up to it from the street. It had, I remember, tinted glass windows, and maybe it was heated in the wintertime. From it opened a beautiful vestibule with tinted windows, built-in cupboards of encarved oak, an enormous dining room,

151

also with tinted windows and built-in furniture, and two rooms on the streetside, each with a leafed door that opened onto a large balcony. Each room had a two-stepped ledge on the left and right side of the balcony; my father called them "lookouts." Fischer furnished one of the streetside rooms as his office; his daughter lived in the other, and they shared the dining room. Fischer and his wife occupied the two-room apartment in the back wing completely furnished with all amenities; it looked out upon the garden, and a stairway led up to it in the back. When they were taken away, it was down this stairway that Vera, his typist, escaped. Also passed on to my father was Irénke's school, consisting of two or three rooms, completely equipped, and also the two-room apartment with all conveniences that belonged to his lover named Margit. (She fled, too.) My father sold off the apartments on Bercsényi Street, kept his office, and moved the furniture to the front part of the Fischers' apartment.

This was the apartment where we arrived with Mami. Egon and Márta Prammer had stayed behind at Várad, but they soon showed up. I don't remember where Márta lived during those first days; I think she stayed with her mother, but they did not get along and squabbled constantly with their joint tenants. For some reason or other, Márta was having dinner at our place. My mother, I recall, served us a bay-leaf potato dish topped with cream; Márta jumped up and spooned the cream onto a platter placed in the middle of the table. I asked if she didn't like cream. "I certainly do!" she said, "but only if it is fresh." "How do you know it isn't?" "By looking at it," Márta replied. I looked at my mother; she didn't say a word.

In the beginning, I lived in one of the streetside rooms, among my own remaining pieces of furniture. I no longer remember how they got there. I settled in comfortably, and I would have felt good if I could have. My mother and Egon lived in the adjoining large room, my father two buildings away in his office. We had become used to his living separately all the time.

Somehow we found ourselves without a kitchen; this was why my mother converted the servant's room into one, so we wouldn't have to share it with Bici and her family. My mother was able to cook even in impossible places.

On one occasion, water overflowed from one kitchen to the other, and Bici did not want to sweep it up, saying it was my mother's fault. Then she took a little broom and swept the dirty water. Some of it splashed into her face. Though she was gentle and good, I recollect that she quarreled relatively rudely, petulantly. I watched the two of them in amazement; the scene was very painful.

We wanted to resume our lives, to get settled somehow. I wanted to enroll in the medical school, but I had to wait until fall. Until then, I tried to make a living with graphology.

Perhaps I still have somewhere a shingle on which was printed, "Alaine V. Polcz, psychodiagnosist and graphologist. Receives at such and such a time." I posted it on the gate. Then Márta related how one time a Sekler man stopped, leaned on his cane, and said, "What does the 'V' stand for? Valiant knight? Man or woman? And what do psychodiagnosist and graphologist mean?"

But my fevers had started up again by then, even though we obtained some Uliron with much difficulty, my mother giving some gold for it. This reminds me that my gold pieces and my jewelry survived, maybe precisely because I did not hang on to them or stand guard over them. In short, I obtained Uliron for gold pieces, and I kept taking it, but the fevers did not abate, and Dr. Mátyás treated me, who had removed my appendix years before.

He ran a private sanitarium; he was a surgeon, internist, and gynecologist, a brilliant professional. He somehow weathered the Jewish period; he was highly esteemed and admired. I remember, a woman stood at a table in his reception room, a pulled-out drawer in front of her containing a stack of money; everyone paid whatever they wanted to. He issued no bills or anything. Mátyás earned a lot this way. Those who did not have any money did not pay anything. Peasant women came who paid ten or twenty pengős or whatever. The pengő was in circulation in Transylvania at the time. (Because of inflation, it was worth less than ten or twenty forints are today.)

Mátyás applied formaline to try to kill the bacteria, but I grew increasingly worse; my fever rose, and my abdomen distended gradually.

I woke up one rainy night. I looked at the furniture; it seemed so familiar; I knew it belonged to me. I looked out the window. Somehow the city was poorly lighted; I did not know I was in Kolozsvár. I sat and pondered where I was, how my furniture had wound up there. I had had "six homes" in this year's time, all of which I, fleeing, left suddenly, within hours with small parcels or suitcases. Even today the feeling haunts me. I wake up in the night and touch the wall and wonder where I am.

Egon got on his own two feet most adroitly. He opened a lawyer's office before long. Márta lived with us all the time; she sunbathed on the terrace in the nude, I remember. The columns above the terrace supported the roof. They were made of marble, or they were painted marbly. She was sunbathing there, and we were conversing. She said the war was over now. (I think the war ended officially in May, after the fall of Berlin.) And what would we do now?

After peace was concluded, the Soviet forces held a big parade in Kolozsvár, too. The parade passed in front of us. The crowd was standing and applauding right and left, Hungarians with greater jubilation, Rumanians with less. A soldier wearing ski gloves in the great heat received especially loud applause. The days at the end of May in Transylvania are very hot sometimes, or maybe it could have been early June already. He had turned down the upper part of their furry lining; it showed white. This made him feel classy. He was happy, he was smiling; he did not realize why he was being applauded. It was a wonderful day for us, too.

At the time, it was not yet decided whether Transylvania belonged to Rumania or Hungary. We stubbornly and desperately hoped that it would be Hungary. The Soviet command was maintaining order; if the Rumanians used violence against the Hungarians, it immediately extended protection. The command was truly making an effort for equality and democracy. It always offered assistance. The Soviet forces represented safety to us in Transylvania.

Despite this, Rumanians did chop off the heads of some young Sekler men with an axe. But we could, we believed, thank chiefly the Soviet forces that even greater excesses and atrocities did not occur. (The Siculicidium[43] has always been in fashion during every era. Like the Jews, the Seklers defied their fate with their toughness, with their bravery.) Of course, when the Russians marched into Kolozsvár, horrid events did take place. The Óvári family episode was mentioned repeatedly. The family lived on Monostor Street; they were a well-known ancient aristocratic family in Kolozsvár. They were entertaining some Soviet officers. It isn't possible to know exactly happened. The fact – this was related by an older woman living in the neighborhood, in whose kitchen a Russian soldier was soaking his feet – is that an officer rushed in and spoke to the soldier, who, while still wet, jumped into his boots and dashed out. On the second or third day, when they entered the Óváry house, they found nine bodies. All the dinner participants, the entire family and one or two guests – every one of them had been shot. Supposedly, the officers had wanted to violate the women, and the men tried to protect them. This roused a very special reaction in me. Horrified, people recounted this occurrence for months. Yet, dear God, the bullet in the head takes a second! A quick, certain, merciful death.

As for what had happened to me, I hardly spoke about it to anyone. This was a different world, people were not very afraid of the Soviet soldiers. I think the tragedy of the Óvári family could well have been an accident.

I would have liked to go and search for János, but I was feeble, feverish. No one would hear of it. It wasn't really possible to communicate with others. But that certain letter and what the Cselkós related had really embittered me. After all that had happened to me, a benumbed terror dwelled within, and only one thing was missing, the consciousness that János had wanted someone else during our honeymoon, that he had infected me.

Márta took to scheming; she asserted that the apartment would be taken from us, and that soldiers had appeared one night, wanting to requisition it; she had rescued our possessions, informing them that she was a doctor and that this was her reception room. I heard their conversation in the stairwell, but only Márta's voice, the soldiers' barely. She persisted until she, with Egon's help, induced my mother to give her my room – of course, with a part of the terrace, the vestibule in front of it, and a kind of sideroom that was also there. Then she settled down and lived in the room with her mother. During consulting hours, Auntie Lina sat out on the "ledge" without making a sound. The outside room, which was formerly the room of Fischer's young typist, served as the reception room, a tiny section adjacent to it as the kitchen. It should not have been a particular problem; after all, this combination reception room and vestibule opened from the stairwell. But it didn't have its own lavatory; there was only one, and that was in the back, for all of us. So Márta and her mother could only go to the lavatory through the vestibule or my room. As to why Márta always chose to walk through my room – without knocking, of course – and her mother likewise, and why I did not speak up, why I put up with it, I don't know.

I didn't have money for medical treatment. Márta recommended a doctor who, at a very great cost and after a long delay, gave me calcium injections. This is what I went to him for, greatly upset. I obtained the money for it from Egon. One time Márta said, "But she is an independent woman, lots of her things are left, she should sell them." I immediately sold one or two items and paid the doctor – the one she had recommended – and gave Egon what I owed him. He felt embarrassed, but Márta came in just then, and, well, he remained silent.

What *was* left? I began to rummage about among my belongings for one or two objects that were especially nice. The enormous lilac-colored, pure-silk shawl with its wonderful hand embroidery and wide fringe and the ashtray made of special crystal, also lilac-colored, that I had received as wedding gifts from Mamika; then those very nice flower pots János gave me; a dark-blue, heart-shaped inkwell and two vases I put in Bici's care at the time. When I asked her to return them, she claimed she knew nothing about them. All the same, they quickly turned up. At that time, a bunch of things remained in my apartment that the Fodors had deposited with me. I did not find any of those objects, either. One time, I asked Éva, "You helped to move my belongings from the apartment. Tell me frankly, what became of them?"

She replied, "Papa Radó put me in charge of selling whatever I could at the flea market."

Well, so my father had sold off all the possessions in our apartment belonging to my mother, him, and his lover named Margit, or given them as gifts to Bici, Éva, and Mac. He had other lovers as well; I believe he gave things to them, too. The apartment also contained many jars of fruit, I remember. It may have been the best year of my father's life. Right in the middle of the widespread hardships after the war, he had three or four apartments to prey upon; he and his lover lived quite merrily. Naturally, he must have worried about us, but that was not particularly his habit. Even at the age of ninety-four he preserved his complete optimism, affability, humor, and irresponsibility.

My condition did not improve; my abdomen grew ever larger; I could no longer fit into my clothes. Regarding this, I had only two dresses, the one I lived in at the front and the one the Soviet soldier presented to me. It was a very pretty dress, and I accepted it: a flowery cotton dress with buttons shaped like daisies. I wore it, but then I gradually could not fit into it; I looked as if I were pregnant. Acquaintances would, I remember, speak to me on the street and ask whether I was pregnant. "No," I would say and be surprised.

Someone related to me that she saw me, as I walked on the street a bit sideways and clinging to the wall, stop before a corner, look to the right and left, and then suddenly dash across to the other side. I believe I brought this way of moving from the front. I couldn't get accustomed to the fact that peace had arrived. To the degree that peace existed in Kolozsvár... Yes, at first it seemed that peace did exist.

I went to Dr. Mátyás. I was lying on the examining table, he flicked my abdomen from the side, it rocked back and forth, "exudative peritonitis." I broke out in a sweat, sat up, and asked, "Why wasn't I told sooner?" He looked at me and said, "What could we have done about it? There is no medicine for it. It is not possible to help. It is probably tubercular."

I looked up an internist. It was established that I also had pleurisy. So I was going for calcium injections while suffering peritonitis and pleurisy, and meanwhile, Márta, the doctor, was living in the room adjoining mine and going through my room to the lavatory.

I resented this as medical negligence. Weeks passed. I was ever less able to walk, I was full of fluid. When I became a bed patient, Márta went to the lavatory, not through my room but through the vestibule. She never came in, never asked how I was feeling.

One time, Ilona Káli Nagy, an old childhood friend, paid me a visit and asked me why I was so full of despair. After everything that had happened, illness completely crushed me. Weakness and fever supplanted reality. I remember, I came home from the doctor, and my mother greeted me so happily that she prepared a place for me to rest on the terrace, but I was depressed and unable to find any pleasure in it. (This hurts me today, I should have displayed some pleasure.)

Poor mother, she did so many things for me. She tried cooking choice morsels for me and put the compresses on my abdomen. She tried to furnish my room lovingly and gently; she wanted to chat, to beguile the time away, but somehow, I was unable to respond to any of it.

But I still attempted something. A cram-course in pedagogy was advertised; I believe, candidates were sent off to employment after an examination in the six-week course. I sailed through the six weeks and had five days to prepare for the examination. I took it. It was not easy. They asked a question like this, for example: What is methodology? I did not even know what the word meant.

I had to pass an examination on the subject of the analysis and practice of music. I was asked what instrument I played. "None." "But you have a good voice?" "I don't." "You do have a good ear, don't you?" "I am tone-deaf." "But you are familiar with scores?" I did not know how to read scores. Despite this, they passed me, perhaps because a work force was needed. Also, my specialized treatise and teaching demonstration were very successful. I had to complete the latter in a Rumanian school, an experimental school. The students were amply aware that a teaching demonstration was going on, that we would not give them grades, that we could not discipline them. They were examining us. They were Rumanians, we were Hungarians. The committee sat to the side on four or five chairs in a circle. I knew Rumanian quite well, but the fever, the illness had greatly debilitated me.

I faced the class and wanted to say something, but nothing in Rumanian came into my mind. That a person was looking the class in the eye and not beginning to speak so surprised the students that they quieted down. When the stillness was perfect, it was, by then, easy for me to begin. It should have been. According to the proper development of the hour, I should have started with a talk, thus ask one of the children what his father's occupation was.

"Zidar," he replied. I asked the second.

"Zidar," he said. The third, too.

Zidar. The fourth, the fifth, the sixth – all said this – bricklayer. Probably they were being impudent. Somehow I kept my presence of mind, and said that anyone whose father had a different occupation should come forward. Not one of them did. At this, I said: It is strange that in this class there are only the children of bricklayers; in other classes, it is like this and that and so on.

The teaching demonstration was successful, and I received my appointment to Magyarvalkó. I became a teacher in the national elementary school there.

Magyarvalkó was a small village; it was without train or bus service and could be reached only by wagon. I would have had to teach four classes. There was no electricity, and I wanted to take a crystal radio and a few books with me. I thought I would dissolve my marriage to János and live quietly there with a clear aim: the preservation of Hungarians and the education of children. After the war, this quietness and tranquility seemed enticing and the responsibility enough for a lifetime: to transport culture, happiness, and entertainment to the end of the world, to a Hungarian village enclosed by mountains.

I still needed one more clearance: the decision of the "purifying political screening committee," that my conduct during and after the war was above reproach or not disputable. I received this, too, and I preserve to this day the appointment and the confirmation document. The appointment is typed on a small piece of worn, coarse paper made of wood fiber; on it are a seal and the signature "Bérczy." The letter 'B' is a bit old-fashioned and fancy.

159

But I never saw Magyarvalkó. Twenty years later, I saw a picture of it in Paris on the wall of a room of an old friend from Transylvania. It showed a small village, with a shingled church with a wood steeple in the center – it lies in the middle of a valley – and flowering trees in the green grass on the hillsides around it. It was a small watercolor.

I did not get there because my illness worsened, and I was told that even if I regained my health, I must stay near the doctor. Then I again thought that if I must remain in Kolozsvár, I would fulfill my old desire to enter the medical university. This stimulated me a little and gave me a certain joy...

My condition continually declined, and I no longer know how, but suddenly I was lying in the Haynal Clinic. It still had an entirely Hungarian medical staff under Haynal's direction. With tubercular inflammation of the peritoneum and the pleura, both with exudation, and probably with socially transmitted gonorrhea.

At first I lay in a general ward. I shivered with cold every day; I had a fever of thirty-nine, forty, forty-one degrees Centigrade; then by morning I suffered exhaustion, subnormal temperatures, and complete prostration. I was suddenly transferred to a private ward. I distinctly remember this, and have written it down elsewhere (somewhere). The room had two beds and loads of flowers. A young woman had died of some throat ailment in the other bed. Her fiancé was taking the flowers away. He looked at me with hatred: I was alive, she had died. "I am also grievously ill," I wanted to say to him; "it is not likely I am going to live." I said nothing. He gathered the flowers up, he left without saying good-bye.

Difficult days followed. I had to cope with my life with the Russians up to that time and the possibility that Transylvania would end up in Rumania – this was as awful as all the other things put together. The information about János...

My illness thwarted me in very many things. I struggled with the fever, with indispositions. I was drowning in accumulated fluid.

I never had any visitors, with the exception of my mother. Later on, Gabi Kiss, my former classmate, visited me and said, "Listen, I have been here twice before, but there is always a sign hanging outside on the door: 'Do not disturb, the patient is asleep.' Are you really sleeping so much?"

I was unable to sleep night or day. During the night fever tortured me, during the day the hustle and bustle of the hospital. I dozed in a strange half-sleep. I endured this half-wakeful state with difficulty. My temperature was normal for a short time after lunch, for an hour or two, and my mother came in regularly and talked with me before the shivers and high fever returned.

As I remember, my father visited me once or twice. I did not feel hurt; he did not like hospitals. Still, the hospital was very near his office and our apartment. Márta never stopped in.

I was lying in the isolation room, and I well knew why. A peasant woman entered, "I want to tell you to ask them to move you out of here because those who are put in this room, they all die."

I found this amusing at the time, and I said, "People do not die because they are put in this room; instead, they are put in this room because they are going to die." Her eyes widened; she looked at me in horror and backed out of the room without saying good-bye.

I immediately regretted saying what I did. Why did I have to say this to her? I learned I wasn't permitted to speak about this. I was not permitted to state that I knew I was probably going to die. (Hereafter I violated this rule only once, in front of Miklós in 1949, again when near death.)

The doctors fought for my life, of course. They tapped fluid by the liters, and they prescribed cardiac restoratives and salicylates in numberless quantities – nothing else was available. Antibiotics did not yet exist. The salicylates made me nauseous, and I was unable to eat. Then they gave me some kind of appetite stimulant; finally they obtained a different medicine to reduce my fever.

A woman doctor sat down on the edge of my bed and persuaded me at some length that I had to eat. I pulled myself together. My mother brought me some paprika chicken; I ate a wing and a couple of dumplings. Then I vomited everything up. I noticed in amazement that the end of the wing remained almost whole as when I bit it off, the dumplings, too. It was as if I had not ingested anything.

I began my "worm" exercises. I shuddered at the thought that if they bury me, worms would feed on me. What strange

161

trivia comprise the components of the fear of death. I did the worm exercises morning, noon and night, and I concentrated intensely on the thought that they were chewing me and that I had to get used to it. Much later, I learned there are no worms in the depths of the grave. (Or are there after all?)

Otherwise, I had such "small" concerns as the following. When János returns home, he won't have a suit of clothes to wear. I thought I would write my last will and testament on a little piece of paper and instruct my family to sell this and that and buy one for him. I also was worried that there would be nothing to bury me in, and I thought I would set down in writing that they should wrap me in a sheet and arrange around me my bridal gown that had survived; then they would not have to worry about what to squeeze me into (my abdomen was so large my clothing no longer fit me). It was complicated, almost impossible to have clothing made after the war. And why should they even take the trouble to do that?

I didn't talk about any of this, I just considered it. I brooded over what had happened, every detail over and over again – the war, the Russians, János, János, János... why did he do this to me? About love, that he was my first... Then the Russians again. Then what would happen to Transylvania. I gradually became angry at God. Within me was a wild rebellion against God, against János. I had never flirted, I didn't love anyone else, only him, and yet he was capable of doing this. Next the Russians, and the war, the deportation of the Jews, the dying soldiers – all this seemed unjust. Inhuman and ungodly. I smile about this today. What kind of justice?

I didn't speak to anyone during these fever-ridden nights and days – and, of course, I didn't speak, I couldn't tell anyone about anything up to that time, either. Some kind of seed had developed from my silence that I could not break open. I did not even want to.

It was at this time that a picture postcard from János arrived. He sent it from captivity, just a few words, something to this effect, "Dear little A, I heard you are sick. Come on, get well, because this is unbecoming behavior. Mercy and sausage. [Sic.]"

When I finished reading it, I was overcome by faintness; I almost lost consciousness. Your heart, your system of blood vessels, your entire being worn out by forty-degree fevers and giddied by subnormal temperatures – you lie there with dazed eyes in the morning and receive a card like this – well, what little strength remains would abandon someone else, too. It abandoned me. I tried not to think about it, but I had to think about it constantly.

Then, I remember, my mother was at my side one night; I became violently ill, my temperature rose to forty-one degrees, the shivers came, the coldness shook my whole body and my teeth chattered, and while my fever soared, my pulse plummeted. Then suddenly my temperature fell to subnormal, and my pulse shot up.

This is called *Totenkreuz*, the cross of death.

It was a magnificent experience; I look back on it with joy ever since, because the following occurred: Everything that hurt so much and seemed so burdensome and beyond all bearing suddenly became distant, weightless, and natural. I have tried frequently to formulate this state of mind and write it down: it was as if until then I had been looking at life through a telescope that brings every single detail close. When I was a child, we would turn the telescope around and even things up close would then suddenly become small and distant. This is what had happened; the telescope had turned around.

I found it meant absolutely nothing that the Russians had dragged me away, that János did not love me, that he had deceived me, that I had hardly lived, that I could not become a doctor. All that meant absolutely nothing; things of this world were not important. This was not despair, not apathy; it was a perception of a different dimension of time. I saw them leading my weeping mother out of the room, I heard the doctors speaking to me. I thought I could reply but did not only because I considered it unnecessary. They gave me injections, massaged me, forced me to breathe – I no longer remember everything they did. I do remember I did not feel the sting, but knew exactly what was happening without taking a look. This liberating, weightless feeling, this perception that it made no difference whether I lived for twenty or eighty years filled me with a extraordinary joy and tranquility. (How unfortunate that this phenomenon is losing its power.)

I almost regretted that the doctors brought me back. It would have been better to die. The next day they said the following, "Well, we were able to bring you back from the other shore this time, but be very careful from now on. We are not likely to be able to do it again."

What idiotic things doctors can say! How can you protect yourself from dying? And why should you not die?

One time, they sent the clergyman to me. I was a Protestant then, so they sent a minister. He stopped in front of my bed with his unctuous text, "My sister, we must always be prepared for the Lord to call on us, and the hour of our death can draw near." I remember I felt highly amused and thought to myself: I know this better than you do. He expressed many more sanctimonious notions and patted me on the shoulder, and I felt he was going to slip his hand to my neck and touch it, caressingly, so to say, and then go lower in the direction of my breast. I felt distinctly that the movement was that of a male. Under the pretext that he was attending to the needs of someone who is sick, in effect gratifying her stifled desires. I had little strength left, but I sat up and declared, "I would like to be alone, I do not want to receive the sacrament, please leave me alone." He continued to talk, and he embraced me to lay me down. I rebuked him, "If you do not leave immediately, I will ring and have the nurse show you out." He looked at me and said, "God does not love an angry person. Blessed and peaceful are the meek. Let us pray together." I let him say the prayer, I thanked him, I asked him not to touch me, and leave.

This experience deepened my loathing of clergymen to the utmost.

And somehow I wound up ever more distant from God. Atheism was approaching. True, but at the time, I was still facing the past and the brutal and painful present in complete loneliness.

There was a Sekler nurse at the Clinic. Her name began with an 'E.' Was it "Etelka"? Maybe. (Her decent, dark-complexioned face and graceful movements are before me even now. She was the same age as I, a nineteen or twenty-year-old woman, a nurse with all her heart. Her sister was also a nurse on the staff, but ill-mannered, dispirited, and peevish.) Etelka told me that whenever I would ring, the other nurses and her sister would remark, "The favorite in the number one isolation room is ringing." (My room number was one.) Why was the number one isolation room a favorite? Because Etelka and I were able to laugh together, even though her life was also bitter. She said little in few words; it is the practice of the Seklers to touch the essential only quite playfully, not to declare something, only to hint at it. I think her fiancé had deserted her, her mother was dead, her father sick. She applied the compresses and assisted when the fluid was being tapped. I remember how well it flowed as she put her arms around me and held me because the water had to be released slowly during the tapping; the fluid shifted my heart toward the middle, and if they had drained it fast, my system would not have been able to bear the drastic change. I lacked the strength to keep myself together, I broke into a sweat, and my entire body shook; then she would kneel before me and hold me until the four or five liters of water drained out of me. After that, I would fill up with fluid again.

I was particularly tormented by the fact that I was not allowed to drink a single drop of water or any kind of liquid. This caused special suffering during thirty-nine or forty degree fevers; I breathed in gasps with chapped lips and cracked tongue. The doctors were unable to come up with anything else. They sent me for radiation treatment to eliminate the abdominal infection. They thought that the gonorrhea was exacerbating the course of the tuberculosis. They put me under the x-ray apparatus on a stretcher, turned the rays on to my abdomen, and left me there. Then they took me back on the stretcher and laid me down in my bed. I did not protest or ask any questions... After the third treatment I became suspicious, and asked what was going on. They said, it was deep radiation therapy. "But won't I become sterile?" I asked Dr. Haynal. "I will not be able to have children because I am sterile?" He replied, "You will never have children, it is not possible to give birth with an abdomen in such a condition."

This filled me with despair. I no longer wanted to live. "But the patient's permission must be obtained for deep radiation, for sterilization," I said. "I do not consent to it." Haynal became extremely irritated; he began to shout, "Be glad we were able to save your life. You are a child, you don't know what you are saying." I sat up, though I wasn't allowed to, and shouted back, losing my patience, "I know medical ethics states that the doctor will do no harm to a patient. My defending my rights did not entitle you to shout at me." He shouted back, "I will not visit you any more!" He left and did not come back. This is what Imre Haynal was like, a wonderful diagnostician and human being. This is what we were like. I became desperate. I would not permit radiation even if I were to die, I told Nurse Etelka. My attending physician recommended that we call in a gynecologist for consultation. They summoned one. He was a very self-possessed individual. He said the following, "This inflammation of the ovaries will keep breaking out; you are not likely to give birth after the tubercular peritonitis and the second case of gonorrheal infection. The professor is right, but speaking humanly, it is not possible to predict anything. The chance is very, very slight, but if you consider giving birth more important than your life, you can refuse to accept radiation."

I refused it.

Haynal did not visit me for a while. The argument and my indignation at their almost making me sterile – or had done so! – somehow roused me. I asked for my case history and looked at the medication I was receiving. I saw it was salicylate, Kalmopyrin, and some kind of appetite stimulant. I called Nurse Etelka and proposed that we now agree to the following on our word of honor. If the salicylate has not helped to this point, it will not help hereafter, either. (It can not help with the peritonitis and the pleurisy.) And evidently because of it, I had no appetite and was throwing up. I wouldn't take any more salicylate. The appetite stimulant didn't improve my appetite; I wouldn't take that, either. We would nicely pour the dosages into the bedpan every day; we would make the tablets disappear somehow.

Nurse Etelka looked at me and asked whether I realized she was risking her job. "And I my life," I replied. We both laughed. Then very secretly, we poured the morning, noon, and afternoon dosages into the bedpan; Etelka ran out with it and then recorded I had taken them on my chart.

One time, my father brought me a bottle of wine and Egon a little canned meat, and my mother made some potato salad for me. I said it was a bit sour and they should pour a little water on it. A little water at long last! I sipped some wine, too. I began eating, and I wanted to live again.

Though I was, of course, still sick and confined to bed, I began to recover my health. I remember the following: I was once given a diuretic injection without being informed. I had to urinate uncontrollably. I rang but the nurse tarried. I somehow crawled from my bed, grabbed up the bedpan, and began to pee. At that moment the door opened, the "entourage" entered, and I could not stop. One of the doctors, despairing, shouted at me, "How did you get up?" He grabbed my wrist, pulled me up, and put me back into bed. I covered my face and asked them to relent, I had to pee. "Here in bed," said the doctor. You are not permitted to get up. Not even to sit up." I felt extremely ashamed of myself; I don't know how it could be that after the Russians, I still was capable of so much modesty.

I asked them to leave the room. They laughed and went out. I lay in bed and it poured out of me desperately; I could not stop it. The nurse entered, Etelka, and examined me, "The diuretic injection is the cause. " She cleaned me up; the doctors came in and said that no matter what happened, even if I released number two in bed, I was not to get up, because who knew what would happen to me then.

Etelka and I looked at each other and smiled. They didn't know that sometimes I would ask her to take me by the shoulders, sit me up, and hold me in that position for a couple of minutes. Then she would lay me back slowly; I would feel better and no problems would appear.

They massaged the bed sores, scrubbed my back, heels and so on with laundry soap. This way I never developed any bed sores.

When I got better, I was given a roommate, a granny. She was grievously ill with pneumonia; she gasped for breath.

I remember that one time they wanted to aspirate me again; I asked them why, when I was so much better. "Didn't you notice you are choking?" the doctor asked. I had not.

During staff visits, the granny was warned to move around a lot, and not lie so motionless. I was delighted at this and spoke up, "Then I have to move around, too, so I won't get bed sores! Why do you keep telling me to lie motionless?" Then Nándor Hun (he has died), whom I have known ever since then (he recently treated Emese, my sister-in-law) said, smiling, "If we tell you to lie without moving, you would still move around too much. If we tell her 'Make sure you move around, dear Granny,' even then she moves very little."

Somehow I regained my strength. My father got hold of a medicine called Rubrofen. It was a red liquid which was supposedly good for peritonitis and pleurisy.

Then they let me go home. I remember, they carried me on a stretcher; no other form of transportation was available. I asked them to cover my face with a diaper or something, but they didn't, and as they carried me on the street – the hospital wasn't far from our apartment, but with a stretcher it still took thirty-minutes – two young Sekler men carried me, they were the stretcher bearers, they put me down time and again so that they could rest. Pedestrians observed me, commented, and felt sorry for me.

They carried me up to our floor. I was home at last.

Of course, I continued to require the compresses, and a woman doctor came to administer the Rubrofen. Occasionally she injected it beside a vein; whenever she did that, she would quickly run away because she had caused me sharp pain. It seemed as if it were ablaze, and I was being cut up with a knife at the same time. Why was it so easy to inject it to the side? Because the red could not be controlled in the red. This pain, however, didn't last more than fifteen minutes. It was so severe that I licked it and bit my arm, though I was inured to pain otherwise. This doctor also had to be paid to come and administer the injection; it never occurred to Márta to do it herself, though she was living in the room next to mine, which she had taken away from me.

A beautiful china dinner set of mine had survived; the doctor and I agreed I would give her the set with service for twelve.

I had to be tapped. Dear Etelka came to do that, and she again held me while the doctors drew and tapped the water from my lungs. My mother brought in a canning jar, then another, and then a pickle jar. They removed several liters then, too. Afterwards I lay exhausted to death; my legs became so numb I thought circulation would never return to them.

I lay in compresses during nights. Bedbugs collected at the edges of the cloth compresses and bit me. My mother fought them fiercely. Márta never came in to see me during that time. My father came up once in a while to chat; he was charming and sweet and asked whether I was feeling better, "You are better, you are looking better!" he pressed me. This annoyed me because I felt I was getting better slowly. You are ill, you are struggling with an illness, you are weary of it, but when others say you are better, you are looking better, you know they are lying, and that is infuriating. (Now that I am occupied with the dying, I make extensive use of these experiences. Of course, sometimes you have to smile at a patient and say, "Come now, you are getting better," but only in rare moments and with a rare smile.)

The summer passed slowly. I began to recover, and since I was no longer allowed to go to Magyarvalkó, I prepared myself to pursue medical studies. Then Nándor Hun came to our apartment and talked me out of it. He said that it was not right to go into medical studies in such a deteriorated condition, that I would not be able to hold up under the strain. He exasperated me – I registered in psychology.

I decided to look up János before the academic year began. My mother and family gave way to despair. Nándor Hun and the other doctors said this was flying in the face of providence. It wasn't easy for them to talk me out of my decision.

The little black cat sitting on my shoulder in an old photograph (the photograph is on the bookshelf next to Miklós's writing table) was called Tilet. I did not know with whom to leave this cat at the time of my flight, and in the very last minute I entrusted her to the janitor of the building next door, giving him a sizable sum to look after her and to feed her. Eventually she wound up with Bici and her family. Tilet, the precious, sweet Tilet, who was so wonderful – Miklós wrote about her in one of his short stories – knew what time at noon I would finish at school, and she would wait for me on top of the gate. She knew I would be arriving at twelve noon on Saturdays and that there was no school on Sunday. She knew when I had physical training and would be staying on. In short, Tilet sat on top of the gate, and when I entered, she jumped onto my shoulder. You could even play hide-and-seek with her. She and I played in the tree branches. Either she would hide and I would look for her, or the both of us would, or I would hide and she would look for me. Likewise in the apartment. How playful she was!

When Erzsi, our Sekler servant, wanted to quit – she always had conflicts with my mother – my father promised her higher wages. She said, "Keep your money, I don't want it. I'll stay just because of the young lady and the cat."

Twenty years later, Erzsi visited my mother in Kolozsvár and was looking at the china. "I say, you still have some of these? I thought I had broken them all."

Later, she called on us in Budapest. She wept. She told my mother that the happiest years of her life were those she spent with us. We used to have a garden with some plum trees and a weekend house on the bank of the Szamos. I was standing under the trees in my blue dress with white embroidery and János approached, and I stood and smiled and waited – he would never forget that picture.

I do not remember whether I was standing there waiting for János, but it's possible that this was where we met for the first time. Irénke, Erzsi, and I were often outdoors, planting potatoes. During the war, edible vegetables had to be planted in flower gardens everywhere. In the end, however, we dug up fewer potatoes than we had planted. Erzsi and I were hoeing potatoes there.

Erzsi had a loyal nature, I did, too. Probably this was why we liked each other. She received word that her fiancé had died. She went out to the promenade on Sunday, returned home, and, weeping, told me about it. But she added, "I do not believe it, I do not believe it! They say they saw him die, but I do not believe it." The young man actually came home, much later. He married her; he beat her constantly. He was given to drinking. He suffered a stroke, and Erzsi diapered and bathed him, then mourned him. She is living with a daughter. She treats Erzsi badly, became an alcoholic, and gave birth to a cardiac child.

"It was never so good for me anywhere as at your place. But I did not know it at the time," Erzsi said. "The war was on, but the front was far away, and we were girls in love."

I have a small, square tablecloth, woven from smaller squares with an embroidered flower in each smooth square. Erzsi did the embroidery. I still have it. This tablecloth made it through the war, her marriage, and mine with János. Only the good Lord knows what I used it for. Did I spread it out for afternoon teas? Or did I wrap bread in it?

I registered at the university in the end. Before the term began, while it was summer, I met Zimra Harsányi. She had come from some death camp, with her hair closely cropped. Her hair was just then beginning to grow. She lived somewhere out on the bank of the Szamos with two boys, who also came from a death camp. I visited them once. Then something happened and they split up. I went to the university with Zimra. István Benedek[44] was our teacher. Zimra wanted to become a writer and submitted her writings to Benedek. He read them and told us that Zimra was without talent and that he would tell her so. He called her to his room, conferred with her at great length, then came out, asked for a clean handkerchief, and took it in. Ten minutes later he came out again, asked for a handkerchief, and took it in. Zimra came out with her eyes red from crying, returned the handkerchiefs, and stopped writing for a while.

She later established herself in Bucharest; she became a famous playwright – with party-line pieces – but then she flopped and developed a loathing for what she was doing, or maybe just the reverse. She came over to Hungary, then went to the West, and I lost track of her. Before leaving, she said, "I was born in Rumania as a woman and a Hungarian Jew. No misfortune greater than this can ever happen to me."

On Lajos Kossuth Street I recognized the woman who had taken in one of Zimra's two young friends, to take the place of a deceased son and take care of. He was sick, a diabetic, and he required nursing care. She heard that I had to go somewhere, to a spa, to quietness, to rest after my illness but did not have the money for it. She tossed a letter with my name written on it that contained two hundred thousand leis into the mailbox. Inflation existed, but even so, this was an enormous amount. I do not know why it occurred to me that she was the one who had sent it to me, but it later turned out that she had. I knew her superficially; I think she once asked for a graphological opinion of the boys. That she whose son had died in camp would give so much – to a Christian woman who, compared to her, was protected – enabled the horror which even then petrified me to ease somewhat for first time.

With this money I went down to Vizakna near the end of summer. I rested and regained my strength. I then registered at the university. At Bolyai University, which sprang up then. That is, the Rumanians took over the Franz Joseph University that year.

Bolyai University opened in a building on Fürdő Street, behind the promenade, that formerly served as a secondary school for girls. At first we sat on packing cases, then we received some benches. Sixteen of us attended psychology for the first year. István Benedek came down, and we also heard lectures by Marcel Benedek and Pál Harkai Schiller.[45] No one had anything. I remember lending a pastry board and dish cloth to the István Benedeks, and a china tea service, and a special, beautiful pot for boiling milk, which I had received as a wedding gift from my Aunt Rózsika (it was like a little bucket, silver on the outside and white enamel on the inside) to Schiller, who later went to America, ran into a tree while skiing and shattered his skull into fragments. This was how we gathered together odds and ends for our university professors, so they could make their lives easier.

Transylvania was awarded to Rumania. For us this was such a blow that people were depressed for days, their heads ached, they felt faint; they had nausea, they could not eat; some lost their voices and could not talk; others suffered from diarrhea or constipation. It was such a blow that we could hardly bear it . But then we tried to recover, we tried to carry on...

EPILOGUE

We cannot even find where our weekend house on the bank of the Szamos was located. A residential district has been built there, panel houses. They are all look the same, you get lost among them. The trees and the soil have also vanished.

They not only removed the graves and the grave markers from the Hászsongárd cemetery, they chopped down the trees in the church graveyard, too. A world has vanished. It has vanished inside me, too.

After the battles blew over in 1945, I escaped from Transylvania across the border to go and see János. He was under house arrest as a political prisoner with Lajos Veress and Géza Lakatos,[46] who, for the sake of the nation, had attempted to pull out of the cataclysm.

Then, as soon as he was set free, I had János slipped into Transylvania, but our desire to remain there was futile, we had to flee. They would not grant a work permit to Hungarians or a passport to go to Hungary. It would never have occurred to me to leave Transylvania; I crossed the border because of János. In Hungary he kept on behaving the same way. He closed himself off from me, chased women, did not hand any money over at home, and hardly spoke to me. It was as if I did not exist at all.

One winter night we were walking along Ráday Street to our sublet room, where we were living with Mami. It was snowing in large flakes, as it had so often in the last year of the war. An iron rod protruded from the corner of one of the buildings. (I can see it now when I close my eyes, it was like the corner of the stove.) "Do you see that? If you leave me, I will hang myself on that," he said.

I left him because I loved him, and I knew it would be the end of me if I stayed with him. It was like extending half an arm, saying, "Cut it off, because if you don't, my whole body will become gangrenous."

And truly, when I left him, I felt relieved. Miklós appeared, but within me was that mortal disease from which he pulled me back, back to life. I was bedridden for three years. I forgot about János. He vanished, sank within me.

He was never able to link himself to someone else. He lived with his next wife for only a couple of weeks.

When he died, his family and Mamika surrounded me as if I were still his wife. Then I learned he had written his last poem to me. But late, in vain. He had ceased to exist within me; he had sunk so deep that his death did not change this situation. I did not understand what became of our great love.

Twenty years later, I dreamt he was coming and wanted to take me with him. I protested that I am another man's wife. I could not go and did not want to. He came anyway, and he appeared in my dreams for days, making demands. We finally scuffled. Then at this moment something within me split apart – as when the ice cracks and water breaks free. He was present again when I was awake – in a different way, of course, but I recalled everything, not the years of our marriage but what had preceded them: Love. The result: Now I no longer dare leave anyone.

But others are leaving me: Auntie Anna, Mamika, Uncle Gábor, my mother, my father, Egon – they all have died. Now, after fifty years, as dictatorships are also perishing, Transylvania is again in travail, and I look upon my wartime marriage as a personal fresco painted on the wall of history.

NOTES

1 "A Transylvanian writer" – author's note. Kádár (1894-1972) founded the Erdélyi Szépmíves Céh in 1924 and served as director of the Hungarian Theatre in Kolozsvár 1933-40. He turned to Protestant theology in 1940, and he settled in Hungary in 1944, where he taught theology from 1952 and edited the *Theológiai Szemle* (Theological Review) from 1958.

2 "A highly reputable ear, nose and throat specialist, my brother's partner" – author's note.

3 "Later, this came to pass" – author's note.

4 József Nyírő (1889-1953) – a Transylvanian novelist and short-story writer, whose works portrayed people living in a state of nature, claiming this state to be the source of human happiness. His writings were strongly influenced by expressionism and filled with strong poetic feeling.

5 "Ildikó Nyírő was directly ahead of me on the class list; we took our oral examination at the same time" – author's note.

6 "A Kolozsvár bon vivant" – author's note.

7 Áron Tamási (1897-1966) – Transylvania writer known for his stories of peasants fighting their landlords, poverty, and nature, often done with much wit and humor. János Kemény (1903-1971) – a novelist, who before World War II, headed Erdélyi Helikon, an organization of Hungarian writers living in Transylvania. The child of an impoverished baron, he was born in Pittsburgh, Pennsylvania, and returned to Transylvania with his family. Miklós Bánffy (1873-1950) – count, member of a noble family that played a major role in the history of Transylvania, politician, writer and dramatist best known for his *Transylvanian Stories* trilogy.

8 Zoltán Jékely (1913-1982) – a poet, writer, playwright and outstanding translator; his translations include the works of Dante, Racine, and Shakespeare. His writings are concerned with philosophical questions. His poems are elegiac and nostalgic, and his early novels are based on autobiographical materials, his later ones on adventure.

9 A play by Emil Ábrányi (1851-1920). Though he wrote a number of successful plays, Ábrányi was better known as a poet and translator, Rostand's *Cyrano de Bergerac* being considered his most successful translation. *The First* premiered at the National Theatre in Budapest on January 13, 1882.

10 "We became closer friends later; his next wife, Aliz Basilides, and I were girlfriends" – author's note..

11 Balázs Lengyel (1918-) – the noted linguist and literary critic and one of the founders of the periodical *Új Hold* [New Moon], the progressive literary and critical journal of young writers first published in July 1946 and banned by the communists in May 1948 for its failure to abide by the principles of socialist realism.

12 "This is how I heard the events occurred" – author's note.

13 "The family of Count Móric Esterházy" – author's note. In 1917 Móric Esterházy (1881-1960) served as Prime Minister for a few months.

14 Lajos Dálnoki Veress (1889-1976) had a successful military career under the Horthy régime. See note 15.

15 Veress was sentenced to death by hanging on April 16, 1947 for "rightist" activities, but the National Council of the People's Court converted the sentence to life imprisonment. He was released during the 1956 Revolution, and he left Hungary and lived out his life in London.

16 "I did so. If a truck was hit, two or three trucks could collide" – author's note.

17 Indivisible and inseparable.

18 Ferenc Szálasi (1897-1946) was Prime Minister under Admiral Horthy, the Regent of Hungary, and head of the Hungarian Arrow-Cross (fascist) Party. He was responsible for the massacre of thousands. In 1945 he fled to Germany, where he was captured by American forces. The Hungarian People's Court condemned him to death as a major war criminal, and he was executed.

19 "I met her once later, at the time of the famine. She had baked muffins and gave me some. Her boy died. Of the three, only one survived" – author's note.

20 "I have just now read its recipe: 'Beat the lightly salted eggs. Mixing it with cream, pour it on the potatoes, then sprinkle grated cheese on top'" – author's note.

21 "The forestry lodges kept in touch; everyone came and went on the various footpaths" – author's note.

22 See note 18.

23 Béla Kádár (1877-1956) and János Thorma (1870-1937) were two outstanding painters of the 20th century.

24 "Kálmán bequeathed his beautiful collection to the museum of the city of Pécs. It can be viewed there today" – author's note.

25 "Naturally, linen was not available during the war, nor after. We pieced out, patched the bed sheets, and sewed two together to make one" – author's note.

26 "I don't speak German, and I'm not going."

27 "Spin the silk, comrade" —from a fifties rallying song empha-
sizing the necessity of working hard to "build socialism".

28 "Russian soldier good, German soldier bad."

29 "I was surprised that Russian officers also sat separately from the
rank and file" – author's note.

30 "It's not working."

31 "The practice was to remove civilians from the firing line" –
author's note.

32 "Maybe this is what was written on the piece of paper" – author's
note.

33 "Thank God it's quiet today."

34 "You don't mind the work?"

35 "Up yours."

36 In Hungarian *"kapu"* means gate.

37 A type of Russian canon.

38 "Dear Madam, you are so kind. You must turn Catholic."

39 The years of hard-line communism hallmarked by the name of
Mátyás Rákosi, First Secretary of the Hungarian Communist
Party until 1956.

40 "Violet will be my wife" – author's note.

41 "Violet did not mean to do it" – author's note.

42 The Hungarian Jacobins were the organizers of the first repub-
lican movement in Hungary. Their leader, Ignác Martinovics,
with six other Jacobins, were executed in 1795.

43 The massacre of Székelys by Austrian troups at Mádfalva in 1764
when they refused to be inducted into the army.

44 István Benedek (1915-1993), writer and son of Marcel Benedek
(see note 45).

45 Marcel Benedek (1885-1969) – renowned writer, translator, and
professor of literature; Pál Harkai Schiller (1908-1949) – a major
contributor to studies in psychology in Hungary. He organized
many psychology institutes and established the Applied Psychology Section of the Hungarian Psychological Association. He
edited the series *Lélektani tanulmányok* (Studies in Psychology)
and contributed several books to the field of psychology. He
settled in the United States in 1947, where he died two years
later.

46 Lajos Veress – see note 14 and note 15. Géza Lakatos (1890-1967)
– Hungarian colonel-general and prime minister (1944) who had
attempted to engineer a separate peace with the Allies before
the German occupation of the country, while continuing to fight
the Soviet forces. He was put under house arrest by Szálasi's
Arrow-Cross in December 1944 in Sopron. He left Hungary and
died in Adelaide, Australia.

Printed in Hungary, 1998

Sylvester János Printing House,
Szombathely